FOOD SERVICE
FACILITIES PLANNING

other AVI books

Food Service

Dairy Science and Technology

Food Science and Technology

FOOD SERVICE FACILITIES PLANNING

by EDWARD A. KAZARIAN
Professor, School of
Hotel, Restaurant and
Institutional Management
East Lansing, Michigan

WESTPORT, CONNECTICUT
THE AVI PUBLISHING COMPANY
1975

© Copyright 1975 by

THE AVI PUBLISHING COMPANY, INC.

Westport, Connecticut

Library of Congress Catalog Card Number: 74-27672
ISBN-0-87055-168-X

Printed in the United States of America

Preface

The food service field has been identified as one of the fastest-growing segments of the economy. The projected demand for food service away from home indicates that an increasing number of new food service facilities will have to be conceived, planned and built in the future. Individuals involved in the planning of food facilities recognize the complexity of the problems of design and the many variables that exist. The understanding and evaluation of these variables as they affect the planning process are important to the eventual success or failure of the proposed food service operation.

The purpose of this book is to present a systematic procedure for the planning of food service facilities. It attempts to identify and describe all the various objectives that have to be accomplished for the preparation of final plans and blueprints. The inter-relationships of various activities as they influence both the construction and operation of the food facility are discussed. Emphasis is placed on describing a total planning procedure that should result in a facility that is acceptable to the customers, the operators and the employees. The significance of productivity as a planning concept is stressed in anticipation of continually increasing labor costs.

It is hoped that this book will serve a dual purpose. It is primarily intended as a text for classroom instruction at the University and the Junior College level. Many educational institutions recognize the importance of planning as related to the development of food service managers. It should also be useful as a reference source for architects, food service consultants, interior designers and others involved in planning food facilities.

This book does not attempt to cover all aspects of the planning process in great detail since many of them deserve a separate volume. However, the overall concepts presented should be considered as prerequisites to further study of many of the subjects presented.

Grateful acknowledgment is extended to the people who contributed their ideas and materials and helped in the preparation of the manuscript.

EDWARD A. KAZARIAN

April 1, 1973

Contents

CHAPTER 1

Introduction to Food Service Facilities Planning

DESIGN AND LAYOUT

The planning of food service facilities is usually a continuous process for those individuals and organizations engaged in the food service industry. The planning involved may be quite simple, as in the case of rearranging tables and chairs in an existing dining room or replacing equipment in production areas. In other cases, the planning may be a very complex problem, such as the development of a completely new food service facility which may involve considerations of land, building design, financing, management policies and operating procedures. Regardless of the complexity of the project, satisfactory results can only be obtained when the planning is guided by the basic concepts and objectives of design and layout.

The terms "design" and "layout" are sometimes confused, and should be clarified to simplify further discussion. "Design" refers to the broad function of developing the entire food service facility, including the original concepts of operation, site selection, menu development, equipment requirements and all the other pertinent planning functions that are necessary to develop the concept into a structural and operational reality.

"Layout" is a more limited function of the planning process that deals with the arrangement of the physical facilities for the food service operation. Thus layout is one of the many tasks that have to be accomplished in the overall design of the facility. It is one of the most important aspects of design because it dictates to a great extent the operational efficiency of the facility.

The entire design of a food service facility includes many functions that are related to the layout function, as well as being related to each other. Some of these design functions can be identified as:

(1) conceptualization of the proposed project;
(2) market studies of a particular area or perhaps finding a suitable location;
(3) financial planning;
(4) location and site considerations;
(5) determining the overall size of the facility;
(6) feasibility studies;
(7) menu development;
(8) merchandising;

(9) service considerations;
(10) development of the dining atmosphere;
(11) organization;
(12) pricing considerations;
(13) food preparation and production techniques;
(14) selection of materials and methods of construction;
(15) layout of equipment, workplaces and aisles.

The order of the listing is not intended to signify the sequence in which they are performed or the importance of the various functions identified. For certain projects, some of these functions are very important to the successful planning of the facility; yet these same functions may not be as significant in other types of projects. For example, the layout function for a drive-in chain that uses basically the same arrangements of equipment and spaces becomes a minor part of design after the first one is planned. In this case, location and site analysis or merchandising may be the more important design functions for the chain. On the other hand, the layout function for an institutional food service facility is very important because of its bearing on construction and operational costs. The food facility planner must sense the importance of the various design functions for each type of project and concentrate his efforts on the most relevant ones.

The design functions identified emphasize the importance of correlating the design and layout of the physical facilities with the operational characteristics of the food service facility. It is common to discuss and evaluate such areas as marketing, menus, labor availability, atmosphere, sales and many others during the planning process.

The design and layout of the workplaces, departments, storage areas, aisles and other facilities should reflect the operational characteristics of the organization. Similarly, it is also true that the existing facilities dictate to a great extent the operational characteristics of the food service enterprise. It is difficult to separate the concepts of design and layout of physical areas and facilities from the basic concepts of good operational procedures and policies. For example, one of the concepts of planning is to simplify the production of food items appearing on the menu. This concept is also a basis for the development of work procedures and training programs for employees. Another concept of planning is to create a physical atmosphere that will attract and retain customers. The same concept is used to develop the merchandising aspects of the operation for purpose of generating sales. Thus it is easily seen that both planning and managing of a particular food service facility are guided by many identical concepts.

In reality, it would be impossible to plan a well-designed facility without a fundamental understanding of basic operational and management principles as they relate to food service operations. Since there is such a close relationship between the physical facilities and the operation of the food service, it is desirable for management personnel to understand the principles of planning, so that the functioning of the operation can be directed as conceived by the designer. Good management is obviously the key to the successful operation of a food service facility regardless of the physical facilities, since good management can overcome poor design and layout to a certain extent. However, a well-planned facility not only simplifies the management of the operation but largely determines the success of the project.

PLANNING

Characteristics

The planning of food service facilities is characterized by some unique design and layout problems that are not commonly encountered in other types of planning projects. This uniqueness is partially caused by the great variety of food service operational concepts that may be used; the variety of customers and users to be served; the material choices available; the production methods possible; and the charateristics of the finished menu items. The fact that a typical food service facility is involved in the production, sales and service of a highly perishable commodity to individuals who must be attracted and pleased contributes to these special problems of design and layout.

One specific problem that the food facility planner faces is the customer or user demand for food service at limited periods of time, which results in peak periods of activity in the facility. These peak periods are obviously the normal meal hours, and the planner must develop a design that will handle these periods with a minimum of effort and confusion. This problem is further compounded by having to plan for different menu items for each meal period during the day, and in some instances even a different type of service for different meal periods.

A related problem that must be solved by the food facility planner is that of efficiently and economically processing and producing all the various food items appearing on the menu in the quantities required. This is especially critical for those operations that have daily menu changes. Some food items on the menu may involve several different raw ingredients or materials which may be available in a variety of forms such as fresh, canned, frozen or dried. The use of different forms of ingredients or materials will require different design decisions.

In addition to considering the menu items, beverages and raw food ingredients involved, the planner is also faced with the design and layout of areas for processing non-food items, such as china, glasses, silverware, utensils and linen, to name a few.

Food facility planning involves designing a system that will maintain the quality of the food items produced. Because of the perishability of many foods, the planner must be sure that appearance, taste, and palatability are not affected by his choice of process or equipment. This is especially critical when prepared foods must be held for a period of time before they are consumed. The design of holding systems for maintaining the desired temperature and moisture content of prepared foods is very important for cafeterias, banquet service and catering operations.

The importance of good planning for food service facilities cannot be emphasized enough. Each new project that involves planning to any extent represents an investment in the physical structure, the equipment, the furnishings, and most important, the continuing cost of the management and labor required to operate and maintain the facility. The result of poor planning is reflected daily in high costs for labor and maintenance and in poor worker morale.

A well-planned facility is developed by utilizing the basic principles from many areas of knowledge. The concepts of work analysis, time and motion studies, human engineering, management, economics, psychology, materials handling, and many other fields can be used advantageously to help plan a food service facility that will meet the objectives of the investors and operators.

In general terms, some of the identifiable characteristics of a well-planned food service facility include the following:

    (1) minimum investment in buildings, furnishings and equipment;

    (2) aesthetic appeal to customers and workers (pleasant dining and working areas);

    (3) maximum profit and return on investment;

    (4) simplified production processes for food and non-food items;

    (5) efficient flow of materials and equipment that may have to be moved about;

    (6) minimum employee travel;

    (7) safe working areas;

(8) minimum waste of time, labor and materials;
(9) sanitary conditions in all areas of the facility;
(10) minimum manpower requirements;
(11) low maintenance costs;
(12) ease of supervision and management.

Much careful thought and planning are involved in developing a design that will meet the criteria indicated above. This necessitates extra time spent in conferences, meetings, research, and on the drawing board. The extra time spent in ironing out the problems of a new plan is probably the least costly investment of the entire project. Many of the above-mentioned characteristics of good design may also be considered as objectives of planning and will be discussed in detail later in this chapter.

Scope

The planning of food service facilities involves considerations of many diverse types of projects dealing with the development and arrangement of spaces, equipment and work areas. The most complex situation is the planning required for the development of an entirely new facility, as illustrated in Fig. 1.1. This type of project requires the planner to utilize both his operational knowledge of the food service industry and his knowledge of the physical planning aspects as related to the facility. Planning a new facility may involve

FIG. 1.1. PLANNING FOR A COMPLETELY NEW FOOD SERVICE FACILITY IS A VERY COMPLEX PROCESS

considerations of location and site selection that may not be involved in other types of projects where the location or site is fixed. If the site is a variable in the planning of a new operation, the planner has an opportunity to do a thorough analysis of the potential market that will enable him to make better design decisions and ensure a successful operation.

The planning of a new facility also enables the planner to make the greatest use of new food products, new processing techniques and new equipment. A more flexible operation can be planned if anticipated changes in products, market, or equipment are considered in the design. Planning a new facility also enables the planner to develop new and interesting concepts of food service merchandising more easily than if he had to work within the restraints of an existing building or of an existing operation. Another aspect of planning a new facility is that it gives the designer the greatest freedom to make decisions regarding the operating characteristics and management policies that should be incorporated into day-to-day operation.

Although planning a new facility is complex, it is a desirable situation because of the many options available to the planner. Other types of projects usually have some type of restriction that the planner has to work around in order to arrive at a practical solution. These restrictions may take the form of existing buildings, which have walls, columns and space limitations that have to be contended with. For example, remodeling of an existing facility is usually done within the confines of the exterior walls for purposes of economy and simplicity. Modernizing is required primarily because of the need for new or greater-capacity equipment to handle new foods, new processes or new techniques of production. Occasionally, a modernizing project is undertaken in the public areas of food facilities to provide a different type of atmosphere or service.

Some remodeling projects involve major structural changes in the building, as occurs when increasing the size of a dining area or when additional production facilities are needed. Projects involving major structural changes give the planner greater flexibility in design, but they do entail considerable cost and possible undesirable interruption of the operation. Whenever structural changes are involved in a project, it is desirable to anticipate any future changes so that provision for making these changes can be incorporated into the design. For example, planning a non-load-bearing wall in the dining room is a good idea if it is anticipated that dining capacity will have to be increased in the near future.

Other types of projects which involve planning include the expansion of an existing production area or department. The ex-

pansion may be desired to increase the production capacity of the department or perhaps to provide faster service. Related to expansion projects are projects that will add new areas or new departments to an existing facility. The addition may be required in order to handle new menu items or a different production process. Sometimes additions are needed to provide a different type of service, such as carry-out or catering service.

Objectives

Every type of planning project regardless of size or complexity is best guided by well-defined objectives. These objectives may be determined by the owner or cooperatively by the owner and various consultants. Written statements outlining the objectives in detail are preferred, so that misunderstandings between owner and planner are avoided.

The general objective for all food facility planning is to make optimum use of money, materials, manpower and equipment to provide the highest quality of food and service. Within this primary objective is the basic concept of assuring customer or user satisfaction. This means that the food service facility has to be designed so that foods can be freshly prepared and be appealing and tasty. More specific objectives of planning include areas relating to either the physical facilities or the operational concepts of the food service, and in many cases apply to both.

Facilitating Production.—As mentioned earlier, one objective common to all types of planning projects is identified as facilitating the food production function. The planner uses this objective to guide the arrangement and layout of spaces, workplaces, equipment and aisles so there is a smooth flow of materials and employees. Management uses this same objective to direct employees in correct work procedures after the facility is built and put into operation.

Materials Handling.—Another objective of planning is to arrive at a design that will minimize the materials handling required in the facility. The planner will utilize many of the principles of materials handling to guide him in achieving this objective. Wherever possible, the planner will visualize the flow of materials through the facility and evaluate many different alternatives of handling these materials. Materials flow in food service facilities includes not only food items but dishes, pots and pans, beverages, bottles, silverware, trash, paper and linen as well. Regardless of the materials involved, it is best to be guided by the precept, "Don't handle materials by hand if they can be handled and moved by some other method." This implies that maximum use of carts, conveyors and other mechanical aids is to be incorporated into the design of the facility. When materials have to be moved, they are best routed over straight-line paths with a minimum amount of back-tracking.

The food facility planner may use many aids, such as product process charts, flow diagrams or string charts, to evaluate and plan for the efficient flow of materials. Some of the basic objectives that guide the design of a materials handling system are:

(1) Minimize the cost of handling materials.
(2) Minimize the time required to handle materials.
(3) Minimize the inventory of materials required to meet the needs of the operation.
(4) Safeguard the materials from deterioration and damage.
(5) Simplify the control of materials used in the facility.

One of the most important aspects of materials handling deals with the standardization of equipment, containers and utensils to be used in the system. Compatibility of sizes in the selection of these materials handling components will result in a simple and efficient system.

Investment in Equipment.—Although maximum use of materials handling equipment satisfies the objective of minimizing the handling of materials, the planner should simultaneously consider another basic objective of planning—that the investment in equipment should be minimized. Thus the planner decides on the basis of economics whether or not it would be desirable to have certain types of materials handling equipment. The basic objective is related to all types of equipment to be used in the facility. Considerations of cost, type, size and maintenance problems associated with equipment are all evaluated before a decision is made.

Space Utilization.—Due to increasing costs of building materials, equipment, labor and construction, the planner must utilize the objective of making economical use of space to develop a feasible plan. This objective refers to both horizontal and vertical spaces and is accomplished by using recommended space standards for workplaces, aisles, storage areas, ceiling heights and shelving. The dishwashing area shown in Fig. 1.2 illustrates some of the concepts of space utilization. Different arrangements of equipment, storage areas and aisle spaces should be evaluated to make certain that maximum use of space is achieved. This objective is not intended to create a facility that is too small and cramped, but instead allows only the space needed to accomplish the essential functions and tasks. This objective is more important for the planning of processing and production areas than for planning for the dining or other income-producing areas. The space requirements for a facility

FIG. 1.2. EFFICIENT USE OF HORIZONTAL AND VERTICAL SPACE IS IMPORTANT
FOR GOOD DESIGN

can frequently be reduced by changing purchasing frequencies, type of raw materials or production processes.

Maintenance and Cleaning.—The provision for maintenance and cleaning ease in the food service facility is another objective of sound planning. The designer considers this objective when specifying materials for walls, floors and ceilings and in the construction methods to be used. The design of equipment is also important in meeting this objective. Providing adequate space for maintaining and cleaning food service equipment is one thing that food service operators appreciate.

Cost Control.—A food service facility designed with cost control as a basic objective will result in a more profitable operation. This, of course, assumes that management will operate the facility with the same objective. Food and beverage cost control is one area where the designer can incorporate many ideas that will keep costs to a minimum. The design of an adequate and properly equipped receiving area where incoming merchandise can be checked for weight, count and quality is very important to this objective. Storage areas can be designed to simplify inventorying and keeping track of expensive food and beverage items. The design of issuing systems is also guided by this objective.

Another area of control that the designer will consider deals with portion control. Design for portion control is reflected by the selection of materials, equipment, utensils and cooking processes that will be used. The availability of preportioned foods has done a great deal toward simplifying the design for portion control, especially for fast-food operations.

Labor Utilization.—A very important objective of planning is to develop a design that will promote the effective use of labor. This objective is accomplished primarily by the design of individual workplaces and work areas. The basic concepts of motion economy, human engineering and work design are utilized by the planner to identify and visualize how the various tasks that have to be performed are to be done. Decisions are made as to the best and easiest way of accomplishing tasks, and from these decisions the appropriate workplaces are developed. Considerations of employee safety, comfort and working conditions are also evaluated and provided for at this time. The physical factors of temperature and humidity control, lighting, noise and air movement are considered as a part of the total design of workplaces. The design of the work area shown in Fig. 1.3 reflects many of these factors. Increasing labor costs demand that more time be allowed for planning efficient workplaces that result in greater employee productivity.

Supervision.—An area that is related to the labor aspect is the consideration of supervision and development of employees. Anticipated methods of training, control and evaluation of performance will influence the design of certain areas in the facility. Operations requiring large numbers of employees may need special areas for meetings, orientation sessions and training programs.

Flexibility.—Another objective that guides the planning of facilities is the concept that provides for flexibility and adjustment to change. In food facilities design, flexibility indicates that spaces and equipment can be easily changed, moved or adjusted to make them more effective for the accomplishment of required tasks. Flexibility leads to better utilization of space and labor. Although this may be difficult to do in some cases, it is an indication of advance planning.

Most of the changes that may influence a food service operation can be fairly easily anticipated. In general, these changes will occur in the materials and products used or in the production techniques necessary to process these materials. The use of partially or fully pre-processed foods is the type of change that can easily be planned

FIG. 1.3. WORKPLACE DESIGN IS IMPORTANT FOR EFFECTIVE
UTILIZATION OF LABOR

for if it is considered during the early stages of the project. Anticipation of changes in menus, portion sizes or service methods can be
envisioned in many cases, and appropriate provisions can be included
in the final design of the facility. Many facilities are planned with
expansion in mind and space for additional equipment can be
provided.

PLANNING IN THE FUTURE

The planning of food service facilities in the future will be influenced by a number of factors that are recognized as critical to the
success of the operation. Such factors as customer appeal, labor
costs and management concepts must be evaluated and properly
planned for. Although these factors were considered in the past,
their importance was not stressed to the extent needed for designing the food service facility for the future.

Customer Appeal

The food service market of the future will be characterized by higher income levels, better education and greater consumer awareness of products and services. For this highly competitive food service market projected for the years ahead, more emphasis must be placed on designing for customer or user appeal. Comfortable, pleasant dining areas, as illustrated in Fig. 1.4, will have to be planned

FIG. 1.4. ATTRACTIVE DINING AREAS ARE IMPORTANT TO THE FOOD SERVICE CUSTOMER

in an attempt to attract and retain a share of the market. Decor and atmosphere are becoming as important as the courteous serving of good food. Rest rooms, lounges and other public areas are also going to be more important to customer reaction and should be planned accordingly. Fig. 1.5 shows rest-room facilities that are attractive and pleasant.

Other concepts dealing with the uses of colors, lighting, ventilation and decor must be incorporated into the design of areas for customer use. The use of these factors in the design of a lounge area is shown in Fig. 1.6.

The future food service customer or user will undoubtedly be more insistent on clean and sanitary facilities; consequently designers should emphasize sanitation in the planning of the operation. There

FIG. 1.5. CLEAN, PLEASANT RESTROOMS ARE A MUST IN MODERN
FOOD SERVICE FACILITIES

will also be increased restrictions in the way of sanitary and safety
codes that will have to be followed. Construction methods, equipment design and ventilation requirements are being stressed more
and more each year in city, county and state building and sanitary
codes. Local sanitarians will probably be more critical in their
evaluation and approval of proposed food service facilities.

FIG. 1.6. LIGHTING CAN BE USED TO CREATE UNUSUAL AND INTERESTING DECOR

Labor Costs

In the past, poor design and layout in the production and service areas could be compensated for by adding whatever additional low-cost help was needed. The projected wage rates and fringe benefits for food service workers indicate that only the efficiently planned, highly productive facility will be able to survive this nemesis of high labor costs. Future food service facilities will have to overcome labor costs by increased mechanization and automation; increased use of convenience foods; better arrangements of production areas; and greater improvements in employee working enviroment.

The incorporation of newly developed equipment, such as silver sorters, conveying systems, change-makers and continuous-process equipment, into the planning of the facility will prove to be important labor-saving factors. Many facilities are using convenience foods to some extent to reduce labor costs. The improved quality and acceptability of convenience foods will result in increased use of these items in the future. The anticipated increase in the use of convenience foods will require changes in the design of areas for storage, production and serving.

Probably the greatest change that will be evident in the future planning of food service facilities is the physical arrangement of spaces and equipment to increase the productivity of workers. A detailed analysis of the tasks to be performed, the best method of performing those tasks, and the planning of suitable layouts will result in the saving of time and labor. Many techniques for generating layouts with the aid of computers are being developed, and these will greatly aid the future planner. The use of computers will allow planners to evaluate many factors in great detail that time did not permit in the past.

Management Concepts

Managers will be a key to the efficient operation of future food facilities. They will be managing employees who have more intelligence and are better trained. Most employees will probably be tending equipment and controls rather than doing strictly manual tasks. They will also be demanding a much more pleasant place in which to work. The fields of human engineering and psychology will have to be used to a greater extent in the design of workplaces and work areas for these employees.

Another trend that management will be faced with in the future is increased union relations. Unionization of food service workers will probably continue to increase each year and require management to be more precise in setting standards of work and performance. More detailed job descriptions and other job-related documents will be necessary to minimize conflicts between labor and management. Careful anticipation of these factors during the planning phase can alleviate many of the problems that could arise after the facility is built and operational.

BIBLIOGRAPHY

BANGS, O. E. 1963. Programming and planning food facilities. Cooking for Profit *32*, No. 10, 48–51, 82.

DANIELS, E. G. 1966. Changes in food service technology and how they affect design. Architectural Record *140*, No. 2, 154–158.

FISK, M., HART, K., and MILLER, G. 1963. Long-range planning for food service layouts. J. Am. Dietet. Assoc. *42*, No, 6, 489–495.

KAZARIAN, E. A. 1969. Work Analysis and Design for Hotels, Restaurants and Institutions. Avi Publishing Co., Westport, Conn.

KOTSCHEVAR, L. H., and TERRELL, M. E. 1961. Food Service Planning. John Wiley & Sons, New York.

LESSMAN, J. 1967. Profitable food and beverage merchandising: the role of design and decor. Hotel and Motel Management. *182*, No. 9, 24–27.

LIVINGSTON, G. E. 1968. Design of a food service system. Food Tech. *22*, No. 1, 35–39.

CHAPTER 2

The Planning Process

The planning of a complete food service facility requires the expertise of many individuals working cooperatively to gather and assimilate the information necessitated by the complexity of the project. It would be impossible to list chronologically all the detailed steps or phases included in the planning process, because many different approaches may be used. There are indeed certain steps that must be completed before further planning can proceed; however, some phases of planning can be accomplished simultaneously or in a few cases independently, depending upon the situation. Actually the planning process can have many starting points, or the various phases involved may be done in a different order.

The various steps of the planning process will be outlined in this chapter and detailed discussions of the more important steps will be presented in later chapters.

The planning process usually begins when there is an idea generated, a desire to be fulfilled, or a pressing need for a food service facility. The project may originate in a market survey which indicates the need for a new restaurant in an area; or a land developer may have a particular location that he feels may be suitable for a food service operation. Some planning projects are created by necessity because they are an integral part of a larger project where food service is desired. Examples include the building of new hospitals, schools, nursing homes and office facilities. Other projects may be created because they are solutions to problems of high labor costs, lack of sales volume or obsolescence in existing operations.

PRELIMINARY PLANNING INFORMATION

After the concepts or ideas for a proposed project have been formulated, the next logical step is to delineate the preliminary planning information and decisions that will characterize the food service facility. This information will be used to guide the overall planning of the project and therefore should be carefully considered. There should be enough detail so that the remaining steps of the planning process can be carried out smoothly. The following points should be considered when gathering and developing the preliminary planning information.

(1) The information is to be used for guiding the overall design of the project, but it does not give all the final answers to all the problems of design.

(2) Information should be general enough to allow for some flexibility in planning.

(3) Information should be specific, on the other hand, on any aspects that are inflexible, such as a fixed site, a fixed budget or a fixed size of building.

(4) Some of the information gathered may be subject to change after further study and research are completed on the proposed project.

(5) The information represents a comprehensive summary of the major objectives and requirements desirable for the project.

In these early stages of the planning process, the information gathered may be presented in outline form. A suggested form for indicating the desirable preliminary planning information is shown in Table 2.1. The form may be supplemented with additional information as required by the particular project to be planned. Some further information may also be gathered during the later stages of the planning process.

The accumulation of this preliminary planning information will help to ensure a more efficient, functional and profitable final design for the food service facility.

PROSPECTUS

Using the preliminary concepts and information gathered in the previous step, the next stage of the planning process involves the development of the prospectus. The prospectus is basically an operational model of the food service facility. This part of the planning process may be completed by the owner, or frequently a food service consultant will be retained to accomplish the task.

In the prospectus, the general and preliminary information regarding the proposed project is evaluated, and fairly detailed descriptions of how the food facility is to function are prepared. Considerable research into the areas of marketing, sales estimating, production techniques, control and management is required to develop a well-prepared prospectus. A brief description of preparing the prospectus is presented here to show its relationship to the other steps in the planning process. This step is so important to the success of the planning effort that a detailed presentation of developing a complete prospectus is presented in Chapter 4.

TABLE 2.1

PRELIMINARY PLANNING INFORMATION FOR FOOD SERVICE OPERATIONS

Type of Project
  New facility   _____
  Remodeling of existing facility   _____
  Expansion project   _____
  Interiors only   _____
  Production areas only   _____
  Others (specify)   _____
Type of Food Service Facility to be Planned
  University or college
    Public cafeteria   _____
    Coffee shop   _____
    Snack bar   _____
    Catering   _____
    Union building   _____
    University club   _____
    Residence halls   _____
  Commercial restaurants
    Table service   _____
    Cafeteria   _____
    Coffee shop   _____
    Drive in   _____
    Take out   _____
    Banquet   _____
    Vending   _____
    Others   _____
  Hospital and nursing homes
    Patient service   _____
    Snack bars   _____
  Hotel, motel, motor inns, clubs
    Dining rooms   _____
    Room service   _____
    Other   _____
  Employee food service
    Cafeteria   _____
    Vending   _____
    Executive dining rooms   _____
    Other   _____
Location and Market Characteristics
  Type of clientele
    Medium income   _____
    Upper income   _____
    Lower income   _____
  Location
    Urban   _____
    Rural   _____
    Suburban   _____
Size of Facility and Hours of Operation
  Number of seats, or   _____
  Total number of people to be fed
    Breakfast   _____   Hours _____
    Noon   _____   _____
    Evening   _____   _____
    Other   _____   _____

TABLE 2.1 (*Continued*)

Menu Characteristics	
Extent	
Limited	_____
Extensive	_____
Alcoholic beverages	_____
Quality and pricing	
High	_____
Medium	_____
Low	_____
Type of Service	
Table service	_____
Booth service	_____
Counter service	_____
Self service	_____
Take out service	_____
Car service	_____
Other	_____
Standards of Service	
Speed	_____
Linen	_____
Paper	_____
Other factors	_____
Type of Atmosphere Desired	
Intimate	_____
Subdued	_____
Formal	_____
Informal	_____
Cheerful	_____
Others	_____
Future Plans	
Expansion capability	
Dining areas	_____
Production areas	_____
Special Features or Requirements	
Parking	_____
Customer facilities	_____
Employee facilities	_____
Special functions	_____
Others	_____

Market

A detailed analysis and description of potential customers or users of the proposed food service facility is the first task to be accomplished in developing the prospectus. Desirable information regarding the market includes items as occupation, age, sex, disposable income, social behavior, consumer behavior, and any anticipated changes in these characteristics. Actually, the more detailed the information regarding the customer or user, the easier it is to complete the other areas of the prospectus.

Menu

The next step in developing the prospectus is to determine the characteristics of the menu that best matches the market described. Menu characteristics regarding frequency of change, numbers of food items in each category to be offered, and the type of food item from the standpoint of a la carte versus complete meals are decided. Other factors include portion sizes, cooked-to-order versus prepared items, or items requiring batch preparation, and any other special features of the menu. Preparation of a typical menu with the suggested format, actual food entrées and portion sizes would be desirable at this stage, because the menu is the key to the development of the rest of the prospectus. All the decisions regarding the menu should correlate with the characteristics of the potential customer in order to maximize sales. The decisions regarding the menu are the most important aspect of preparing the prospectus, since most of the other decisions regarding the design of the food service facility are dictated by the menu.

Service

The next area to be considered in preparing the prospectus is determination of the type of service to be offered in the facility. This is decided by evaluating both the market and the menu in order to select the most appropriate type of service or combination of types of service, if more than one is desirable. Consideration of service standards is also appropriate at this time.

Type of Food Service Facility

The decisions regarding the market, the menu and the type of service can now serve to characterize the particular type of food service facility to be planned. The description can be stated in very general terms, such as cafeteria, coffee shop, specialty restaurant, or drive-in. The classification of the type of food service facility enables the planner to utilize specialized information available for such operations and simplifies completing the prospectus, as well as the remaining steps of the planning process.

Atmosphere

At this point in the development of the prospectus, the concept of the type of dining atmosphere to be developed for the facility is decided. The atmosphere is described in general terms that convey an image as related to the consumer, the menu and the type of service. Food service atmosphere may be identified by such terms as formal, informal, cheerful, friendly, relaxed or appealing. The creation of the dining atmosphere is accomplished by proper selection of colors, furnishings, wall and floor coverings, lighting and by careful control of temperature, relative humidity, noise and odors. Costuming and attitude of employees are also important to the development of a desirable dining atmosphere. A separate chapter is devoted to discussing the creation of atmosphere because it is so critical to the success of a food facility.

Operating Characteristics

The description of the market, the decisions regarding the menu and the type of service also lead to identifying the operating characteristics of the food facility, which is another component of the prospectus. Operating characteristics to be determined include days of operation per year, hours open per day, seasonal variations expected, and the expected meal loads per meal period or during peak periods.

Other operating characteristics described in the prospectus include the type of organization and management policies under which the food facility will operate. These can be briefly described by the type of ownership and an organization chart showing departmental breakdown. Control concepts and procedures, merchandising methods, public relations, maintenance, and personnel development are included in this part of the prospectus. Any special operational concepts that may be unique to a particular food facility should be adequately emphasized so that appropriate planning decisions can be made.

Feasibility Information

An essential part of the prospectus deals with the financial aspects of the proposed food facility. This obviously is a very critical point in the planning process and should be prepared as carefully as possible. In some instances, the feasibility study is done separately from the prospectus by a qualified consultant. The information pertaining to the market and the operational characteristics of the proposed facility are evaluated in relationship to a particular site or location. The concept of facility size in terms of number of seats or number of meals is determined as well as preliminary space estimates for the building. These are used to estimate income and costs. Seat turnover and check averages are used to develop sales volume for the facility.

Expected food and beverage costs are developed and estimates of labor, overhead and other operational costs are prepared. A proposed budget, projected cash flow, return on investment and other financial considerations are also estimated in order to evaluate the feasibility of the project. Chapter 5 is devoted to a detailed presentation of making the feasibility study because of the importance of this aspect of planning.

After the prospectus has been completed, it is reviewed to make sure that all the concepts are workable and that the information presented is as accurate as possible. If all aspects of the prospectus, especially the financial considerations, are satisfactory to the parties concerned and it appears that the proposed project can be economically undertaken, then the planning process can continue.

COMMISSIONING PLANNERS

Armed with the prospectus, the owner or his representatives can approach and evaluate the individuals who will make up the planning team for the project. Hopefully, the selection of the architect, the food service consultant, and other members of the planning team will be based on their ability to develop the plans and specifications from the guidelines presented in the prospectus. Architects and consultants will show prospective clients completed projects they have done for others, so the owner can make an intelligent choice. After selection and commissioning of the architect and other consultants has been completed, the detailed planning of the proposed project can begin.

The key members of the planning team will meet with the owner or his representatives to outline the necessary planning tasks. At this meeting, the prospectus is again reviewed to make sure it contains all the information necessary for the various members of the planning team. It is not uncommon for certain parts of the prospectus to be altered at this time to take advantage of ideas and concepts that may be presented by the planning group. Professional food service designers are usually the best source of advice and judgment regarding a proposed project because of their experience and knowledge about the food service field.

Whenever a group of individuals is involved in the planning process, some of whom work independently, it is advisable to have a written understanding of what functions each member of the group will undertake and be responsible for. This will eliminate duplicated effort and assures that the planning team will work effectively together.

DEVELOPING THE CONCEPT

This phase of the planning process involves identifying or visualizing the various functions and tasks that must be performed to meet the objectives of the food service facility. It is necessary, not only to develop detailed space and equipment requirements, but also to aid in the final arrangement and layout of the facility. Identification of the functions also simplifies the gathering of the data required for proper planning of the entire facility. The functions are determined by using the prospectus, especially the proposed menu, as a guide. Examples of common functions identified for food facilities are purchasing, receiving, storage, preparation, processing and serving. These functions are related to the production of menu items and are easily identified. Auxiliary or supportive functions, such as warewashing, trash and garbage disposal, maintenance and sanitation, should also be identified. Management functions of control, planning, supervision and evaluation, to name a few, are to be included as well.

Requirements for both guest and employee convenience are also identified as necessary auxiliary functions: parking areas, waiting areas, washrooms, locker facilities, office space, and training facilities are examples of these.

A related step in this aspect of the planning process may be described as task analysis. For each function identified, there are certain basic tasks to be performed. An evaluation of these tasks generates the data needed to determine space and equipment requirements. To illustrate, consider the receiving function. The basic tasks involved include counting, weighing, determining quality, moving materials and checking orders. These may be accomplished in different ways depending upon management policy and operational procedures. The method of performing each task is evaluated by considering the materials involved, type of equipment that may be used, and the skills required by the employees. This may require considerable data-gathering and research before deciding on the method of performing the task. The data are obtained and summarized so the planners can make appropriate decisions regarding the design of work areas to be developed.

EQUIPMENT REQUIREMENTS

Equipment requirements are best determined from a complete analysis of typical menus. For each food item on the menu, information regarding anticipated number of portions to be prepared, portion sizes, batch sizes, main ingredients and the processes to be performed are indicated. Much of this information can be taken directly from the recipes for each of the menu items. If recipes are not available, the food service consultant will rely on his knowledge of production practices to generate the information.

From the production processes identified, the planner can then decide whether equipment is to be used to complete a particular process or whether it can be done manually. If equipment is to be used, the planner will then evaluate the type and capacity required. At the same time the various types of equipment are selected, the total time that the equipment will be used for each process is recorded. The specific time of day that each piece of equipment is to be used is also recorded. After this is done for each process, the equipment usage is evaluated and final equipment capacity can be determined.

At this point in the planning process, it may be found desirable to add, delete or change some of the menu items or processing methods in order to achieve greater equipment utilization. For example, if a steam-jacketed kettle is required to process two menu items but is operated for a short period of time, additional menu items may be suggested to utilize the equipment more fully. Another solution would be to change or eliminate the two menu items, thus eliminating the need for the steam-jacketed kettle. In this manner the food service planner can maximize the usage of the equipment.

SPACE REQUIREMENTS

Another phase of the planning process deals with the determination of space requirements. This aspect is related to equipment selection because of the space needed for placement of equipment. Space requirements are also dependent upon the functions and tasks that have to be performed in the facility. The space required is best determined by considering all the factors involved, including the floor space needed for the employee; working surface space for manual tasks as illustrated in Fig. 2.1; aisle space for movement; equipment space; provisions for storage of hand tools and supplies; and provision for storage of incoming and outgoing materials. This aspect of the planning process may be thought of as the development of workplaces or work areas for each task. As these workplaces are developed, the estimation of time requirements for each task enables the designer to possibly schedule several similar tasks to be performed at a given workplace. There are certain workplaces that can be used for only one task because of sanitary or other reasons.

As these individual workplaces are developed, consideration is given to the overall operation of the facility, so the grouping of individual workplaces into larger work areas or departments results in a feasible solution. Thus the planner is designing the individual workplaces and the total space for the facility simultaneously. This part of the planning process is completed when the space required for all the functions and tasks has been determined.

FIG. 2.1. SUFFICIENT WORKING SURFACE SPACE HAS TO BE PROVIDED FOR MANUAL TASKS

DEVELOPING PRELIMINARY PLANS

The next phase of the planning process involves preparation of preliminary sketches and drawings for the facility. This is referred to as the schematic design phase of the planning process. Ideas relating to the building structure, the site, and the location of various facilities, such as parking and receiving areas, as related to the building are developed and correlated with the arrangement of interior spaces. At this point, several feasible solutions may be generated, and these are presented to the owner for approval or selection. Many planners use ideas and concepts from existing operations that they know are workable.

The preliminary plans usually include floor plans showing the general arrangement of equipment, aisles and functional area locations. Frequently, pictorial views of selected areas are prepared, to provide a better grasp of the final design. Elevation views are used to depict size and shape of the building or to show cross sections of parts of the building.

All drawings and sketches are prepared with the intent of conveying ideas and concepts, and therefore are quite tentative. There may be several changes made before a plan is acceptable to the individuals involved.

Cost Estimates

Although it is impossible to determine exact costs this early in the planning process, preliminary estimates should accompany the sketches. These include cost estimates for the building, site preparation, equipment and furnishings. These costs are usually estimated on the basis of square footage or cubic footage of the building.

PREPARATION OF FINAL PLANS

Upon approval of the preliminary sketches and drawings, the next step of the planning process involves the development of the specifics of the design. The equipment capacities, workplace design, door sizes and locations, aisles and other similar details are finalized and blended into a finished layout for the food facility. Many planners use templates or scale cut-outs of equipment and areas, as shown in Fig. 2.2, to evaluate possible arrangements and configurations. This is the phase of the planning process where the layout function is emphasized. Upon approval of the final layout, structural details, building materials, utility requirements and distribution, and a multitude of other details are decided upon and put into plans and specifications.

The final set of plans that are drawn are referred to as working drawings. They are drawn to scale and dimensioned to show sizes and locations of equipment and areas. These plans will be used for construction and installation purposes and must be accurately prepared. Accompanying the working drawings are the written specifications for construction and installation.

PREPARING SPECIFICATIONS

Specifications are a written description of the proposed project. The specifications are intended to complement the working drawings and to clarify any items that may be questionable. To illustrate, the working drawings contain notations which are short, general, and describe a type of equipment or construction method. The specifications expand on the characteristics of the materials involved and the workmanship desired in installing them. A notation on a drawing may simply read "2-compartment stainless steel sink." The specifications will completely describe the sink and establish such details as type of stainless steel, construction of the joints, degree of finish, type of supports, and many other characteristics of design.

The specifications present a complete written description of the total project in an orderly and logical manner. They are used for estimating costs and for the preparation of bids by construction contractors. A complete set of specifications will expand and clarify the working drawings; define precisely the quality of materials, equipment and workmanship; establish the scope of work to be performed;

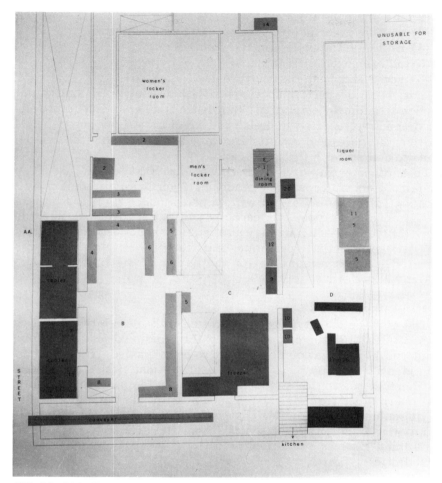

FIG. 2.2. SCALE CUTOUTS ENABLE PLANNERS TO GENERATE SEVERAL ALTERNATIVE LAYOUTS

and spell out the responsibilities of the prime construction contractor. There are several types of specifications that may be written including performance, descriptive, reference, proprietary and base-bid.

Performance Specifications

Performance specifications describe the work to be done by the results desired. For example, the performance specifications for a building roof will establish the following areas:

(1) character and arrangement of the various components;

(2) materials and finishes;

(3) roof loads including wind loads to be supported;

(4) provision for expansion and contraction;

(5) allowable deflection;

(6) acceptable heat-loss coefficients.

This type of performance specification allows the contractor enough freedom to employ his knowledge and experience to provide the desired results. He will design and select the various components, provide the necessary structural members and assemble the components to comply with the specifications.

As another example, a food service consultant knows that many manufacturers are capable of producing fryers with different characteristics. He may choose to write a performance specification that will establish the type, size, capacity and output per hour that will meet his requirements. He may also require manufacturers to submit test data certifying the performance of their fryer. Now the manufacturer becomes responsible for the design of the fryer to ensure that it will perform as specified.

Descriptive Specifications

The most detailed type of specification is the descriptive specification. It describes the components of the building or piece of equipment and how these components are to be assembled. The specification identifies the physical properties of the materials, sizes of each component, spacing of supporting members, sequence of assembly, and many other requirements. The contractor has the responsibility of obtaining or constructing the work in accordance with this description. In this type of specification, the architect, engineer or consultant assumes the responsibility for the performance of the final design.

Reference Specifications

Reference specifications employ standards of recognized agencies and authorities to specify quality. Some agencies and authorities frequently mentioned in specifications include Underwriters Laboratories, Inc., American Standards Association, American Society for Testing Materials, and the National Sanitation Foundation.

Many companies state in their literature and catalogs that their products or equipment conform to specific recognized standards. Most food service equipment, for example, is manufactured according to the standards set up by the National Sanitation Foundation. Electrical components are commonly built according to the Underwriters Laboratories' standards. The user is thus assured that such equipment will meet certain minimum requirements and he can expect a certain degree of reliability and performance.

Reference specifications are generally used in conjunction with one or more of the other types of specifications. For example, in addition to specifying the performance of a fryer, a reference specification can be included that would indicate that the fryer has to conform to the National Sanitation Foundation standards.

Proprietary Specifications

Proprietary specifications call for materials, equipment or products by trade name, model number and manufacturer. This type of specification is the easiest to write because the commercially available products and equipment set the standard of quality that is acceptable to the specification writer. One disadvantage of proprietary specifications is that they may permit the substitution of alternative products and equipment that may not be exactly the same. Under a proprietary specification, the designer is responsible for the performance of the products and equipment.

Base-bid Specifications

The establishment of acceptable materials and equipment by naming one or more manufacturers and fabricators is referred to as a base-bid specification. The bidder, under the specifications, is required to prepare his bid with prices submitted from the suppliers mentioned. The base-bid specification will usually permit a bidder to substitute for the specified materials or equipment providing this is acceptable to the architect or owner.

Base-bid specifications provide a great degree of control over the quality of the materials and equipment.

Regardless of the type of specification to be used, this difficult and time-consuming task is the most important aspect of preparing documents that guide the construction of the proposed facility.

BIDDING AND AWARDING CONTRACTS

On large projects involving building construction, the final drawings and written specifications are made available to contractors who are interested in submitting bids. On smaller projects, different arrangements for the work to be done can be made. For any project to be put out for bids, a standard set of documents, including bid forms, forms for bonds, insurance requirements, instructions to bidders and legal considerations, is available. Most architects use the documents entitled "The General Conditions of the Contract for the Construction of Buildings" prepared by the American Institute of

Architects as a guide for preparing these forms. Separate bids may be taken for food service equipment.

When bids are received, the architect and other consultants involved in the planning will review them and make recommendations for the awarding of the contract for construction. If the drawings, specifications and bidding documents are complete, the lowest bidder will usually get the recommendation. This does not have to be true in cases where the bidder has made exceptions to the specifications in preparing his bid.

After the construction contracts are signed, the contractor will make detailed roughing-in drawings for all utilities to be used in the facility. These drawings are referred to as shop drawings and are checked against the architect's mechanical and electrical drawings. The shop drawings are approved before actual construction begins.

CONSTRUCTION

During construction, the architect and food service consultant periodically check and evaluate the progress of the project. The completed building is accepted only after the architect has made a final inspection and is satisfied that all work has been completed as specified.

The finished facility will reflect the pains taken during the planning phases. If the planning was done carefully, the result will be functional, productive and aesthetic. Careless or haphazard planning, on the other hand, usually results in a facility that will be inadequate for efficient food service operations. It is too late to think about the importance of good planning after construction has been completed.

BIBLIOGRAPHY

ANON. 1960. Checking written "specs." Volume Feeding Management *15*, No. 11, 64.

BANGS, O. E. 1968. A master plan for food service design. Kitchen Planning *5*, No. 1, 19–21.

McCABE, J. 1968. The five phases of professional planning. Kitchen Planning *5*, No. 2, 50–53.

MOORE, J. M. 1961. Plant Layout and Design. Macmillan Co., New York.

WATSON, D. A. 1964. Specifications Writing for Architects and Engineers. McGraw-Hill, New York.

WOODMAN, J. 1964. The anatomy of food service design. Institutions *54*, No. 1, 69–71.

CHAPTER 3

The Planning Team

MEMBERS

Most large food service construction projects are planned by a team of individuals working cooperatively to achieve the final plan. Each member of the planning team supplies his own area of expertise to the project. The typical primary members of the planning team for a large project include the owner or his representative, an architect and various members of his staff, and a food service consultant. In some projects, additional members, such as interior designers or landscape architects, may be involved if there is need for their specialized services. Some architects who do a lot of food service projects will have food service consultants and other types of consultants on their staff. However, the owner is free to use an independent food service consultant or other outside consultants if he so desires.

In some cases, special consultants may be included on the planning team to handle problem areas of planning. These consultants may specialize in accounting methods, marketing, legal aspects, lighting systems, colors, acoustical methods or structural design. The work of any of these special consultants is generally coordinated by the architect.

Smaller planning projects that do not involve major construction or structural building changes can be handled without the services of an architect. The remodeling of dining areas or production facilities, for example, may be entirely handled by a food service consultant. Some large food service organizations have their own planning department and do not require outside architects and consultants.

Regardless of the nature or size of the planning team, each member has certain tasks and areas of responsibility. These may be undertaken by the team members themselves, or they may assign or arrange for others to do the actual work under their supervision. For example, architects frequently will hire lighting engineers to plan and design the lighting system for the facility. However, the architect, who is responsible for this area of planning, must approve the work of the lighting engineer.

Owner

The owner or his representative is a key individual in the planning team, since basically all design and planning decisions must be approved by him. The owner is usually responsible for seeing to the completion of the planning functions outlined below. (Frequently the owner will rely on others to do the actual work involved, but he must still approve and bear the responsibilities for these areas.)

(1) Develop statements of basic goals and objectives for the project.

(2) Develop the basic operational concepts for the food service facility.

(3) Assure that all legal and other regulatory restrictions that may influence the project have been checked out or cleared before too much time in planning is committed. This includes the areas of deed restrictions, codes, zoning ordinances and licensing that pertain to the construction and operation of the food facility.

(4) Complete the market analysis (this is frequently done by outside consultants hired by the owner.)

(5) Decide or approve all financial matters such as procurement of investment capital, financing methods, interest rates and payment schedules.

(6) Complete and approve the feasibility study. (Feasibility studies are often done by accounting firms specializing in food service operations.)

(7) Develop policies regarding standards of operation for the food service facility. The owner may rely on a food service consultant's advice on this matter.

(8) Select the architect and/or other members of the planning team.

(9) Select and approve designs and plans submitted by the various members of the planning team.

(10) Approve and sign contracts. (May use services of a legal advisor.)

Architect

The architect is another key individual in food facility planning and coordination. All projects involving the new construction of public spaces have to be planned or approved by a licensed architect. The complexity of planning a new food facility has cast the architect in the role of an editor who has to coordinate, develop, select and supervise all the various phases of planning. Some of the areas of responsibility of the architect, with his staff of engineers and other supporting individuals, are the following:

(1) site planning considerations such as building orientation, traffic patterns, parking areas, service areas and the location of entrances and exits;

(2) topographical changes required for drainage;
(3) building design from the standpoint of shapes and configurations;
(4) structural design of floors, walls, roofs and ceilings;
(5) exterior treatment of walls, windows, entrances, exits and roofs (Fig. 3.1);

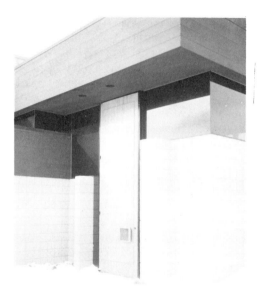

FIG. 3.1. EXTERIOR DESIGN OF THIS BUILDING SHOWS
AN INTERESTING CONCEPT FOR AN ENTRANCE

(6) interior treatment of floors, walls, windows, doors and ceilings;
(7) selection of building materials;
(8) determination of construction methods to be used;
(9) checking building and construction codes for acceptable materials and construction methods;
(10) design of the central heating system;
(11) design of the ventilation system;
(12) design of the plumbing and water system;
(13) design of the air-conditioning system;
(14) design of the lighting system;
(15) coordinating the work of food service consultants, interior designers and any other consultants working on the project;
(16) preparing plans and blueprints for the facility (the food ser-

vice consultant usually prepares the plans and blueprints for the kitchen and dining areas only);

(17) writing specifications for materials and construction methods;
(18) developing cost estimates;
(19) preparing bid documents;
(20) analyzing bids for construction;
(21) checking shop drawings provided by contractors;
(22) inspecting construction of the building and installation of equipment.

Selection of Architects.—Early in the planning process, the owner will select the architect to perform the above-mentioned tasks of planning. Selection of the architect is a very important matter, which must be done carefully if the owner expects to get the type of facility he wants. The selection of an architect usually begins with a list of prospects whose names may be obtained from various sources. It is best to seek out architects who specialize or do a good portion of their work in the food service field. Checking with other food service operators who have used the services of architects is one way of developing a list of prospects. Another source is the local chapter of the American Institute of Architects. Before deciding upon an architect to do the planning, the owner will want to consider a number of points relating to the ability of the architect. The following areas are sometimes used as a basis for selection.

(1) the design philosophy and creative ability of the architect to develop an aesthetic facility;
(2) the engineering design philosophy that the architect follows;
(3) experience and reputation for designing food service facilities;
(4) professional ethics;
(5) size and type of staff;
(6) reputation for completing scheduled work on time;
(7) methods of researching and specifying new materials and equipment;
(8) cost consciousness;
(9) accessibility to specialized consultants;
(10) recommendations of satisfied clients;
(11) ability to work with other consultants.

The matter of fees is also important in the selection of an architect. Architectural fees are usually quoted on one of three different bases:

(1) a percentage of the total construction cost;
(2) a lump sum, for which the project scope must be clearly defined;
(3) cost plus a percentage fee.

Architects charge additional fees for extra services, such as conducting feasibility studies, changes in plans after they have been approved or for special drawings and models. They may also add a fee for the coordination of outside consultants that are brought into the project.

Food Service Consultant

The food service consultant is an individual who is familiar with all aspects of food service operation. He is especially knowledgeable in the areas of menu planning, service, food merchandising and the handling of food through the various storage, preparation, processing, and cooking steps. The food service consultant should also be familiar with management principles, the design of food service equipment, and have a general knowledge of architecture, engineering and interior design.

The food service consultant is responsible for the design of all aspects of the food service operation and consequently must work closely with the architect. Obviously the owner and architect together should select a food service consultant that is satisfactory to both. The best time for this selection is when the architect is commissioned.

The food service consultant may advise both the owner and the architect on certain aspects of the total design of the facility. He specifically, however, is involved in the following areas of responsibility.

(1) development of the menu including food items, portions, prices and format;

(2) determining methods of service for food and beverages;

(3) creation of the dining atmosphere (usually with the help of interior designers) (see Fig. 3.2);

(4) determining functions and tasks to be performed in the food facility, including the selection of materials and processes;

(5) development of control procedures for food, beverages, cash, linen and other materials;

(6) preparation of potential profit and loss statements and budgets for the food service based on projected sales and costs;

(7) advising the owner on preferred operating policies;

(8) determining specific items of food service equipment to be used in the facility;

(9) determining adequate space requirements for all the food service functions to be performed;

(10) developing efficient space arrangements and layouts for the facility including dining areas, as illustrated in Fig. 3.3;

(11) development of operational instructions for the use of the

FIG. 3.2. CREATION OF PLEASANT DINING FACILITIES IS ACCOM-
PLISHED BY DESIGNERS

food facility and especially for the use of the food service
equipment;

(12) preparation of cost estimates for the food service aspects of
the facility;

(13) preparation of all plans required for installation of equipment
in the dining and production areas;

(14) checking equipment design for safety features and ease of
cleaning;

FIG. 3.3. ARRANGEMENT OF TABLES AND CHAIRS IS A PART
OF THE FOOD SERVICE CONSULTANTS' RESPONSIBILITY

(15) writing specifications for all items of food service equipment, furnishings and supplies;
(16) determination of utility connections and capacity required for the food service equipment;
(17) checking contractors' shop drawings for all food service equipment installations;
(18) inspection of equipment installation;
(19) coordination with architect on information required for preparation of the bid documents;
(20) helping in the analysis of bids.

In general, the food service consultant deals with all aspects of design except the architectural, structural and general mechanical work that is done by the architect. The close cooperation that is needed between the architect and the food service consultant is evident by the overlapping of their respective responsibilities in the design process. The wise owner pays as much attention to selection of the food service consultant as to choosing the architect.

The services of a food service consultant may be obtained from independent consultants or from individuals associated with manufacturers or suppliers of food service equipment. Many of the independent food service consultants are identified by their membership in either the Food Facilities Consultants Society or the International Society of Food Service Consultants. Both groups admit only members who are not associated with equipment manufacturers or suppliers.

Food service consultants generally work under one of three payment methods. One method is based on a percentage of the cost of food preparation and service equipment; this cost is based on all equipment that is specified by the food service consultant only, and does not include any items specified by the architect. The second payment method is a cost-plus arrangement where the consultant will provide his services on the basis of a multiple of his actual costs involved. A third possible payment method is a per diem arrangement where the consultant is paid for the total number of working days devoted to the project.

SPECIALISTS ON THE PLANNING TEAM

The owner, the architect and the food service consultant are the main members of the planning team, and most food service projects are completely planned by these individuals. In projects where special requirements are needed or where special emphasis is to be placed, other individuals may be called in as members of the planning team.   Some of these, and the contributions they can make toward the planning of the food facility, are indicated below.

Land Developers and Realtors

Land developers and realtors are involved in those projects that require the acquisition of land or space for the proposed food facility. Food service facilities are frequently a part of a larger development, such as shopping malls, apartment complexes or office buildings, and land developers will sometimes seek out food service operators to install and operate these facilities.

The land developers and realtors are well versed in zoning ordinances and can be valuable in selecting sites or spaces for a food facility.   Their knowledge of land values, future developments and identification of growth areas of a community is useful in making decisions regarding a particular project.

Interior Designers

The services of interior designers are required when special emphasis is to be placed on creating a unique building interior. Interior designers will usually work with architects in developing the following areas:

FIG. 3.4. SELECTION OF WALL AND FLOOR COVER-
INGS IS AN IMPORTANT ASPECT OF INTERIOR DESIGN

(1) selection of furniture for the facility;
(2) selection and coordination of interior wall and floor coverings (see Fig. 3.4);
(3) development of the color scheme for all interior surfaces;
(4) treatment of windows (drapes, shades and curtains);
(5) selection of lighting fixtures;
(6) selection of decorator items, including items for dining tables such as tablecloths, china and silver;
(7) creation of special lighting effects;
(8) development of shapes and sizes for areas and rooms by the use of dividers, plants, balconies, etc. (Figure 3.5 shows the use of a partial divider to create an intimate dining space);
(9) selection of uniforms for employees.

FIG. 3.5. USE OF PARTIAL WALLS CAN ADD TO THE DESIGN OF DINING AREAS

Landscape Architects

A landscape architect may be needed for projects demanding special treatment of the grounds surrounding the food service facility. Among the services that are contributed by landscape architects are the following:
(1) development of the total landscape plan for the facility;
(2) selection and arrangement of trees, shrubs, and flowers;
(3) development of lawn and garden areas;
(4) design and placement of exterior lighting;

(5) development of exterior pathways;

(6) enhancement of desirable exterior building features.

Although a landscape architect may be selected after the building has been constructed, it is desirable to hire him at the same time other consultants are retained so that he can contribute to the overall planning of the facility.

CONTRACTING FOR SERVICES OF PLANNERS

Formal agreements are usually made between the owner and the other members of the planning team. In most cases, a single contract between the owner and the architect is sufficient. Under a single contract the architect will assume responsibility of all aspects of planning regardless of the members involved. He may have other consultants on his staff which would be covered under the single contract, or he may sub-contract the services of other consultants. In projects where an architect is not required, the owner may work through a food service consulting firm and sign formal agreements with it.

The usual architect's contract calls for the architect to prepare and submit to the owner for his approval all preliminary studies, sketches, drawings and specifications. The architect is also expected to assist in the selection and procurement, at the most economical cost, of all equipment required for the food service facility. He will help in the selection of bidders, prepare bid documents and be the general guardian of the owner's interest in obtaining all necessary permits and licenses. Filing of plans with appropriate authorities is also a part of the architect's responsibility.

The contract stipulates the architect's fees and the method of payment. Payments are usually spread over the duration of the project, a lump sum becoming payable when the drawings and specifications have been completed. The remainder of the fee is paid in installments as the project progresses. A set sum in the neighborhood of 10% is held out for a specified period of time after the completion of the building. This is not paid until all approvals of the project have been obtained from the public authorities having jurisdiction. The contract also contains a provision for the situation where the project is cancelled or abandoned by the owner, and for the payment to the architect in such cases. It is also desirable to have provisions for arbitration of any dispute that may arise between the owner and the architect.

Relationships Between Planners and Contractors

Although the general contractor who will construct the food service facility is not considered a member of the planning team, an understanding of his responsibilities and his relationship to the architect and the owner is helpful in discussing a total project.

The owner will carefully study the complete set of bid documents before requesting bids from contractors for the construction of a new facility. These include all the working plans, drawings and specifications prepared by the architect, the food service consultant and other consultants involved in the project. The owner should check them against the concepts and ideas that were developed during the preliminary phase to see if they will result in the type of facility desired. The owner is also advised to consult with a lawyer regarding the legal aspects of submitting the project for bids from a number of contractors. After the owner is satisfied with the bid documents, the job will be put out for bids with hopefully the lowest bidder being selected to construct the facility.

There are several types of contract arrangements that can be made between the owner and the contractor. Some of the more common arrangements for the construction of buildings are as follows:

(1) a lump sum contract;
(2) a fixed ceiling price based on time and materials plus a fixed fee;
(3) a fixed ceiling price based on time and materials plus a percentage fee;
(4) time and materials plus a fixed fee.

Each type of contract has its advantages and disadvantages. However, under a detailed set of plans and specifications, there will not be a great deal of difference between them. Under all the time and materials contracts, all the labor and materials used in the construction of the facility should be audited by both the contractor and the owner or his representative.

Standard agreement forms for the construction of buildings are available from the American Institute of Architects and are recommended for all large projects. The forms available include the following:

(1) the standard form of agreement between owner and architect;
(2) the standard form of agreement between contractor and owner for construction of buildings;
(3) the general conditions of the contract for the construction of buildings.

Under a construction contract, the general contractor is required to accomplish and be responsible for the following areas:

(1) performing the work and furnishing the materials and equipment as defined in the plans and written specifications;

(2) complying with the regulations and ordinances of public authorities having jurisdiction over the project;

(3) obtaining all necessary permits and all certificates showing satisfactory completion of the work;

(4) furnishing the required public liability and compensation insurance;

(5) completing the construction of the building on or before a predetermined time, or paying a penalty for failing to do so;

(6) guarding against charges for extra work, labor and materials (such charges should be authorized only by the architect or the owner);

(7) removing all trash and rubbish caused by the contractor's work from the premises;

(8) maintaining adequate protection of all his work from damage and protecting the owner's property from injury or loss.

Payment to the contractor is made in installments as the work progresses. As with the architect, a certain sum is withheld for a specified period of time to assure that the project has been completed in accordance with all plans and specifications and has been fully approved by all parties concerned.

In summary, the planning and construction of a new food service facility involves many individuals who have to work very closely to enable the project to progress satisfactorily. Unnecessary delays by certain members of the planning team will in turn delay the completion of the plans and specifications. Likewise, delays in construction are also undesirable and should be avoided whenever possible.

BIBLIOGRAPHY

BRENER, S. W. 1966. Pre-construction advice for prospective owners. Hospitality 5, No. 9, 34.

BROTEN, P. R. 1966. Buying the job: how to deal with contractors. Cornell Hotel Restaurant Admin. Quart. 7, No. 1, 39–48.

JARRET, W. R. 1966. How to work with architects. Cornell Hotel Restaurant Admin. Quart. 7, No. 1, 29–38.

ROBERTSON, B. E. 1968. The kitchen planner as a systems analyst. Kitchen Planning 5, No. 2, 37–39.

CHAPTER 4

Preparing the Prospectus

IMPORTANCE

The preparation of the prospectus or operational model is one of the first important steps that have to be completed in a planning project. A carefully prepared prospectus defines what the owner desires and expects in the food service facility. It enables the architect, food service consultant and other planning team members to plan and design the facility efficiently. The prospectus will include management objectives as well as decisions that will affect the operation of the food service facility. Experience has shown that the more detail there is present in the prospectus, the easier the remaining planning steps become.

Since the prospectus is the guide to planning, it is possible and sometimes even desirable to change the information or decisions as planning proceeds. Changes may be made that reflect new ideas or concepts that are developed as more information is gathered for the project. These changes should always be made with the objective of improving the final design.

The suggested areas of information to be included in the prospectus will be presented in outline form. The outline is primarily intended for commercial food service facilities; however, it may be used for other types of operations. It is important to indicate that there are considerable inter-relationships between the various factors included in the prospectus.

CUSTOMER AND USER CHARACTERISTICS

A preferred method of starting the prospectus is to investigate and describe the potential customer or user that the food service facility will be designed for. The desirable information to be gathered and identified is indicated by the following categories.

Occupation

Identification of customer or user occupation is important to many of the planning decisions that are to be made for other parts of the prospectus. This information is also used in some of the later stages of the planning process. Development of the menu, portion sizes, method of service, pricing and type of dining atmosphere to be created are all dependent upon adequate identification of the occupation of the potential customers or users. Occupational data for a given area may be obtained from census reports or from local chambers of commerce. A suggested listing of descriptive occupations commonly used to describe customers or users of food service facilities is given below.

  (1) business people including manufacturers and retailers
  (2) clerical workers and office workers
  (3) craftsmen
  (4) homemakers
  (5) laborers
  (6) professionals
  (7) retired individuals
  (8) sales personnel
  (9) service workers
(10) students

Most planning projects will be designed to attract a particular occupational group. There may be certain food service projects that have to be designed for more than one occupational group. In this case, a percentage breakdown of occupations can be estimated to show the distribution.

Income Level

Information on annual income levels can also be obtained from census and chamber of commerce reports. In addition, several periodicals including *Sales Management* and *Fast Food*, devote an issue annually to market information that includes either total income or disposable income. The information from these various sources is usually expressed as per capita income or as family income. Needless to say, the higher the income level, the more there is available for eating out. Food service facilities designed for high income level customers can obviously be more elaborate and of higher quality.

Income data for the prospectus may be expressed as a percentage of individuals or families who fall in given ranges or groups. A typical breakdown of income ranges or groups is shown below.

Under $4000	$12,000–13,999
$4000–5999	$14,000–15,999
$6000–7999	$16,000–19,999
$8000–9999	Over $20,000
$10,000–11,999	

The food service facility to be developed in a particular location has to be correlated to the income levels present.

Age

Knowledge of the ages or age groups of potential customers and users is needed for the development of the menu and dining atmosphere. The type of food items to be placed on the menu, the portion sizes and prices must be matched to the particular age groups, to ensure attraction and retention of customers. Teenagers and young adults are very atmosphere-conscious and this is frequently the influencing factor in deciding where to dine.

Census reports can be used to gather age data for particular locations. Suggested age categories for use in food service planning are as follows:

Under 5	27–39
6–12	40–52
13–19	53–65
20–26	Over 65

The age information can be expressed as percentages or numbers of people in each age category.

Sex

The food service facility that is designed primarily for one sex or the other will have a distinct character. For example, facilities designed for female clientele would be characterized by pleasant atmosphere, large and comfortable rest rooms, unique decorations, and menus that feature specials, salads and sandwiches. Portion sizes can be smaller also.

Facilities designed primarily for males will be less formal and feature different menu offerings in larger portion sizes. The design of food facilities that cater to both sexes will necessarily blend these characteristics.

Education

The educational level of the potential customer has been identified as an important factor in dining-out habits. Generally speaking, the higher the educational level, the greater the frequency of dining out. Education also appears to be a factor influencing the variety of menu items desired and the willingness to try new or different foods.

Motivation

Knowledge of the motivation people have for dining out can aid planners and managers to develop and operate a successful food facility. Some of the motivating factors are identified below.

(1) change in routine (a favorite of housewives);

(2) necessity due to time or distance limitations;

(3) convenience;
(4) business reasons;
(5) social, such as meeting or entertaining friends;
(6) special occasions, birthdays, anniversaries;
(7) adventure;
(8) entertainment and enjoyment;
(9) to obtain special kinds of meals that are not usually available to the home market.

These motivational factors for dining out are used to develop and guide the overall merchandising and public relations programs for the food facility.

Spending Habits

The spending habits for dining are related to occupation, age, income and other factors and are very difficult to measure accurately. An analysis of spending for other items such as cars, appliances and luxuries of life will be indicative of how much people will spend for dining out. In general, the amount of money spent on meals away from home is increasing in all segments of the population. This is especially true of the younger generation.

Activities that Relate to Dining Out

Another important guide to the overall design of the food facility is found by determining the activities that potential customers will be involved in. Only those activities that relate to dining out need be considered. Many of these activities reflect a particular location or area and may not be meaningful until a definite site for the food service facility is being considered. The typical activities that can be related to dining out are:

(1) shopping
(2) traveling or touring
(3) attending conventions
(4) visiting
(5) business meetings
(6) entertainment events (sports, shows, theaters)
(7) organized group meetings
(8) meetings of social groups

Evaluation of these activities will determine the desirability of designing special facilities such as banquet rooms, cocktail lounges and meeting rooms for the proposed food service operation.

Arrival Patterns

The size of dining tables, seating arrangements and serving times are among the design considerations that are determined by arrival patterns of potential customers. Arrival patterns will influence the design of the facility from the standpoint of peak periods of operation. An estimate of the numbers or percentages of each of the groups indicated is needed for these purposes.

(1) singles   (4) men groups
(2) couples   (5) women groups
(3) families   (6) mixed groups

Additional information in terms of arrivals per unit time can sometimes be estimated and are of great help in planning. Knowing the number of people to be fed per hour or per minute will pinpoint many of the design decisions needed to plan the food facility. Arrival patterns may also be estimated by statistical characteristics such as the normal distribution or the Poisson distribution.

Miscellaneous Factors

For any given project, there may be other factors of customer or user knowledge that can be useful for design purposes. Their importance and need are best determined by the owner or the food service consultant. Some of these additional factors are identified as follows:

(1) ethnic background
(2) food preferences or types of meals desired
(3) eating habits
(4) service preferences
(5) marital status
(6) means of transportation
(7) preferred meal periods for dining out
(8) preferred days for dining out

Much of this information regarding the customer that is gathered is used to develop the remaining parts of the prospectus. The information is critical to proper development of the menu, the type of service, the atmosphere and the operating characteristics of the food facility. The development of these other areas of the prospectus should be closely correlated with the characteristics of the market to be served.

DEVELOPMENT OF THE MENU

The development of the menu for the food facility should be done carefully because it is the foundation upon which the layout and other design functions are based. The menu serves as the source of information for the various food items that are to be prepared and consequently the processes required for their preparation. The processes, in turn, determine the space and equipment requirements for the facility. In addition, the menu guides the decisions that are made regarding the merchandising policy developed for building and maintaining sales.

The owner or food service consultant will develop the menu by keeping in mind the effect it has on other design decisions. In essence, the development of the menu evolves from considerations of the market, ease of production and the layout required. These areas are then used to arrive at the final decisions regarding the planning of the total facility. The menu also has a bearing on the type of personnel, their training and the supervision needed to produce the various food items.

A brief discussion of the basic considerations for developing the menu for a proposed facility will be presented. The prospectus should not be considered complete unless it includes a sample menu.

Frequency of Change

The first decision to be made in developing the menu is to determine the frequency of change. This may vary from a completely fixed menu to one that changes daily. Considerable thought has to be given to this decision because of its relationship to the remaining phases of the planning process. Planning a facility for a fixed menu is much simpler than for a daily-change menu. Daily-change menus are required for many types of institutional food services; however, commercial operations are free to develop any type of menu characteristics desired. It is possible to have an operation that has a fixed menu for one meal and changing menus for the other meal periods. A common arrangement is to have a fixed menu for breakfast and changing menus for lunch and dinner. Some of the categories of frequency of change for menus are described in the following.

(1) *Completely fixed menu.* Many fast food and specialty operations use completely fixed menus. The only changes that are made occur when a menu item is added or dropped for popularity, profitability or production considerations.

(2) *Fixed menu with seasonal changes.* This variation of the fixed menu is used to accommodate the availability of seasonal food items. Most operations using this type of menu will change twice a year, a few making as many as four changes a year. This is not usually a complete change of menu items but primarily those items that have seasonal popularity.

(3) *Fixed with changing specials.* This is also a variation of the fixed menu. The specials may be changed daily and are indicated clearly on the menu. This type of menu is used when

the simplicity of a fixed menu is desired but consideration of repeat business leads to changing special food items.

(4) *Complete daily changes.* This type of change is best for an operation which has decided upon offering a very limited number of food items on the menu and has heavy repeat business. This type of menu is also desirable for operations catering to captive customers, as in some resort or camp operations. This concept may be used by seasonal food service operations that are open for a limited period of time during the year.

(5) *Cyclical daily changes.* This type of menu change is used in operations catering to repeat or captive customers as exemplified by employee cafeterias, educational feeding operations, and institutional food services. The cycle is usually from two to six weeks in length. Seasonal variations can also be incorporated into this type of menu.

(6) *Daily changes with standard items.* This is basically a daily change or cyclical daily change concept with the addition of some popular short-order items. Steaks and chops are common standard items with this type of menu.

Type of Menu Offerings

Another consideration in developing the menu is to decide on the type of menu offerings. The usual choices are a la carte items or complete meals. Most individuals prefer a la carte offerings although some market segments are inclined to favor the complete meal. A happy medium is to have the combination of a la carte and complete meals. Another possibility is to offer complete meals for one meal period, perhaps breakfast, and a la carte for the other meal periods.

Extent of Menu Offerings

A very critical decision regarding the menu is determining how extensive the menu offerings should be. In the total food service market, there is a place for all types, from the very limited offerings of small operations to the extensive choices available in deluxe table service operations.

A limited menu is desirable from many standpoints, including simplified planning for the facility and simplified production of the few items. The limited menu will require less equipment and space in the facility. Its drawback is that it may not attract enough customers to make the operation profitable.

The more extensive menus require more precise planning and are more difficult from the standpoint of production; they also result in slower service and require more equipment and space in the facility.

They do attract a larger segment of the market and are desirable for this reason. Fortunately, many areas can support food service facilities of both types.

The extensiveness of the menu items can be modified somewhat after the operation is opened and a better feel for the customers' desires is obtained. It is better to avoid drastic changes in the menu after the facility has been planned.

The suggested offerings shown in Table 4.1 for each category of foods for a dinner menu may be useful in deciding how extensive a menu to develop. Similar tables of foods may be developed for other meal periods.

After deciding how extensive the menu offerings should be for each meal, the next step is to select the particular food items that will appear on the menu. The following factors are considered in selecting a particular food item.

(1) *Popularity or sales appeal* as related to the identified market. This area is very critical to the success of the operation. Food items that are proven sellers should be selected, but not exclusively. Some variety of foods is desirable so that customers are not subjected to menu monotony and fatigue.

(2) *Profitability of the foods*. This requires an analysis of the foods that would yield the greatest net profit after food, labor and other costs are considered. Profitability and popularity are not necessarily found in the same foods and the menu should reflect a balance between them. A menu composed

TABLE 4.1

SUGGESTED FOOD ITEMS FOR MENU DEVELOPMENT

Appetizers	Beverages
Canapes	Coffee
Cheeses	Fruit drinks
Cold cuts	Hot chocolate
Egg rolls	Milk, chocolate
Fruit cocktail	Milk, whole or skim
Marinated herring	Shakes and malts
Pickles	Soft drinks
Relishes	Tea, hot
Shrimp	Tea, iced
Bread and Rolls	Desserts
Biscuits	Brownies
Bread, rye	Cakes
Bread, white	Cheesecake
Corn bread	Cookies
Hard rolls	Fruit
Hot rolls	Gelatin desserts

TABLE 4.1 (*Continued*)

Bread and Rolls (*Continued*)
Muffins
Packaged crackers, garlic toast, etc.
Sandwich buns
Toast

Entrees
Beef
Chicken
Chili Con Carne
Chopped beef
Eggs
Entree salads
Fish
Frankfurters
Ham
Macaroni and cheese
Meat balls
Meat loaf
Noodles
Pot roast
Pork
Shrimp
Spaghetti
Turkey
Veal

Sandwiches
Bacon-lettuce-tomato
Barbecue
Cheese
Cheeseburgers
Chicken salad
Club
Corned beef
Egg salad
Fish
Grilled cheese
Ham
Hamburgers
Hero
Hot dog
Roast beef
Steak sandwich
Turkey or chicken
Tuna salad

Vegetables
Asparagus
Baked beans
Beets
Broccoli
Brussels sprouts
Cabbage
Carrots
Corn

Desserts (*Continued*)
Ice cream, sundaes
Pies
Puddings
Tarts

Potatoes
American fried
Au Gratin
Baked
Boiled
French fried
Hashed brown
Mashed
Scalloped
Sweet potatoes

Salads
Cole slaw
Cottage cheese
Fruit
Gelatin
Lettuce
Tomato
Tossed salads

Soups
Bean
Beef bouillion
Celery, cream
Chicken
Chili
Clam chowder
Consomme
French onion
Minestrone
Mushroom
Potatoe
Tomato
Vegetable

Green beans
Lima beans
Onions
Peas
Rice
Squash
Spinach
Tomatoes

entirely of highly profitable items would certainly not be the most popular.

(3) *Method, ease and speed of production.* How smoothly a kitchen functions is a direct result of this factor. Foods that are easily processed require less time, labor and equipment. Fully pre-processed and portioned food items represent one way of achieving the same result for foods that are difficult to process. Another alternative that leads to simplified production is to select short-order items that are processed on only one piece of equipment.

(4) *Sources of supply and variations in supply.* A constant source of supply is desirable for all food items that will appear on the menu, but this may not always be possible for certain foods. If source and reliability of supply appear to be a problem for a particular food item, it is best not to include it on the menu. Each food item that is put on the menu affects some aspect of design, and wise decisions at this point of the planning process will simplify later planning steps.

(5) *Manpower required to produce the food item.* Considerations of skill, training required and the availability of qualified personnel to prepare food items should be evaluated. It makes little sense to put a food item on the menu that cannot be produced with high quality consistently.

(6) *Equipment requirements and usage.* A set of food items appearing on the menu that meet most of the above-mentioned criteria and still balance equipment workloads is an ideal situation. This can only be achieved by a careful analysis of the type of equipment required by each food item and the usage time needed to process the number of portions to be prepared. This analysis can be done after the menu has been developed to see if full equipment utilization has been achieved. Many food items can be modified slightly to make better use of equipment.

(7) *Portion size.* Portion sizes are determined from the standpoint of appearance, cost, price and variety. Some portion size variation among the food items appearing on the menu is desirable to satisfy those who are inclined to be small or big eaters. Visual appearance of the food item is the main consideration in determining portion sizes. The portion size and the number of portions to be prepared are needed before equipment capacity can be determined. Typical portion sizes for a variety of food items are given in Appendix A.

(8) *Compatibility.* Food colors, textures, aromas and visual appeal

are important factors in evaluating food items for compatibility. Food service operations offering complete meals should be particularly careful of choosing food items that go well together.

(9) *Pricing.* Customers like to be given a sense of menu range and value. This can be accomplished by adding a lower-priced item or two to the menu. This tends to suggest fairness and excellence of higher-priced menu items. It is also important to consider pricing in relation to consumer spending patterns.

The importance of carefully developing the menu can not be stressed enough. The menu sets the character of the food service facility. It influences the size, design, layout, equipment, merchandising, operating procedures, and, most important, the projected profits. Since the menu is also the key to equipment utilization and balanced work scheduling, its influence is felt long after the facility has been planned and built.

SERVICE

The type and standards of service for the food facility are determined in the light of the potential customer and the menu offerings. The service has to be compatible with these factors in order to create a unified design. Although there is room for considerable variation in types of service, most individuals quickly relate certain menu offerings to service expectations.

Types

Generally, there are two basic methods of service to consider for food facilities. These are referred to as service units and self-service units. Service units provide waiters or waitresses or other personnel to serve the food directly. The principal types of service units are table service, counter service, booth service, tray service and room service. The design and operational considerations related to each type of service unit are evaluated before a decision is made.

Table service operations with waiters or waitresses are preferred by those who wish to relax and enjoy a leisurely meal. The general table service operation as shown in Fig. 4.1 requires more square feet of space per seat than the other types of service units.

Counter service is suited to individuals who want a quick meal with a minimum of fuss. It is ideal for breakfast and luncheon operations that have a limited menu and desire a high turnover of customers. Counter service operations require a minimum of space because the preparation and service of food is done in the same area.

Booth service operations are usually preferred by teenagers, young

FIG. 4.1. TABLE SERVICE RESTAURANTS REQUIRE
AMPLE SPACE FOR THE SERVICE FUNCTION

workers and travelers who want some privacy while eating. The use of booth service is recommended for medium-priced facilities that hope to cater to a large segment of the market. Both limited as well as fairly extensive menus can be used with this type of service.

In an attempt to appeal to a greater variety of people, combinations of table, counter and booth service units may be used in a single facility. The number of seats to provide for each type of service is dependent upon the arrival patterns of customers. Counter and booth service units are not used for larger groupings of customers.

Tray service units are used primarily in hospitals, for airline feeding and for drive-in operations. Special design is required for the assembly, holding and distribution of foods in these types of facilities.

Room service is a specialty type of service unit for hotels, motels, motor inns and resorts. Facilities for this type of service require separate areas for loading the room-service carts.

The principal types of self-service units are cafeteria service, buffet service, take-out service and vending units. Self-service units are selected when quick service to a large number of people is required.

Cafeteria service units are suited to busy shoppers, business people and families. Low- to medium-priced prepared meals are usually featured, although cook-to-order sections can be provided.

Buffet service can be combined with other types of service units or it can be used by itself. Some operations may decide to use buffet service for a particular meal, such as breakfast or lunch, and another type of service for the other meals. Buffet service is very suitable for special days or occasions where larger than normal crowds are anticipated.

Take-out service has become very popular with low-priced, limited-menu operations. It is appealing to a large segment of the market because it fills the need for a quick meal. This is evident by the growth of franchised take-out operations.

Vending units are ideal for between-meal snacks or for limited-time meals in schools, institutions and industrial plants.

Selecting the type of service unit for the facility should be done carefully since, like the menu, it influences many design decisions. The type of service to be provided will determine the type of serving equipment and serving personnel required. The planner will also have to evaluate the flow of service personnel in the serving or dining areas.

Provisions for the service of beverages may also be evaluated in this part of the prospectus. This is important if it is anticipated that alcoholic beverages will be sold.

Other aspects relating to service that are identified at this time include the standards of service desired in the food facility. The selection of table coverings, dishware, glassware, and flatware should reflect the menu and the method of service. The decisions regarding these items should be made early in order to provide a simple and unified design.

ATMOSPHERE

Another important facet of preparing the prospectus is to identify the desired dining atmosphere for the food facility. For planning purposes, a brief description of the type of atmosphere as related to the customer, the menu offerings, and the method of service should be given. In a sense, the menu offerings and the method of service will characterize the atmosphere to some extent. These two factors, when matched to the expectations of the potential customers, will provide the clues as to the type of atmosphere to be planned. For example, if the prime customer group consists of women shoppers, offering a medium-priced menu with cafeteria service is a natural. The provision of a dining area that is quiet, colorful and attractively decorated will complete the bill.

Since many factors make up the dining atmosphere, probably the easiest way to identify it at this stage of the planning process is by descriptive characteristics. Common terms used include formal, informal, quiet, rushed, noisy, cheerful, pleasant, relaxing, colorful, festive and intimate. If any special feature such as the location, a unique building shape or a theme is to be emphasized, it should also be identified as contributing to the desired atmosphere. Early identification of the atmosphere is helpful to all members of the planning team since it can affect all aspects of design and layout. Exterior

FIG. 4.2. EXTERIOR DESIGN IS AN INTEGRAL PART OF THE CREATION OF A PARTICULAR ATMOSPHERE

design, as illustrated in Fig. 4.2 is important in conveying a quick impression of atmosphere to the customer.

OPERATIONAL CHARACTERISTICS

The operational characteristics of the proposed food service facility are identified by many items of information. Most of the operational characteristics are determined by the food service consultant and are based on experience and knowledge of successful methods of operation. Among the items of information required for completing the prospectus are the following:

(1) ownership;
(2) legal organization;
(3) days and hours of operation;
(4) expected numbers of customers;
(5) procedures for purchasing, production, service, warewashing, waste disposal, trash disposal, customer ordering, waitress ordering, maintenance and cleaning;

(6) control methods for costs, purchasing, receiving, storage, issuing, portions, cash, payroll and security;

(7) personnel requirements and policies;

(8) accounting practices;

(9) special functions for training, supervision and management;

(10) employee and guest facilities.

Regulatory Considerations

The regulatory considerations are also included in this part of the prospectus because many of them have a direct bearing on how the facility is to be designed and operated. Examples of the items that have to be checked to see how they might influence the proposed project are listed below.

(1) minimum wage laws, both state and federal;

(2) employment of women and minors;

(3) anti-discrimination laws;

(4) labor laws;

(5) sanitation codes;

(6) building codes including electrical and plumbing;

(7) licensing requirements;

(8) income taxes; federal, state and city;

(9) withholding and social security taxes;

(10) employment security taxes.

Some of the above items will directly affect the design and layout of the facility while other items apply primarily to the operating procedures. It is desirable to evaluate both areas carefully because of their relationship to the success of the proposed facility.

Since the development of the prospectus is deemed so important an aspect of the planning process, a suggested format for recording the information is given in Appendix B. This format can be used for most projects; however, additional data may be required for very special cases, which can be gathered as needed.

BIBLIOGRAPHY

BANGS, O. E. 1966. The new food service operation. Cornell Hotel Restaurant Admin. Quart. 7, No. 1, 9-14, 21.

BRODNER, J., MASCHAL, H. T., and CARLSON, H. M. 1962. Profitable Food and Beverage Operation, 4th Edition. Ahrens Publishing Co., New York.

CHASE, R. M., and COMPTON, R. A. 1966. The operational model in food service planning. Cornell Hotel Restaurant Admin. Quart. 7, No. 1, 22-23, 38.

DYER, D. A. 1971. So You Want to Start a Restaurant? Institutions/Volume Feeding Management Magazine, Chicago.

VAN DRESS, M. G., and FREUND, W. H. 1967. Survey of the Market for Food Away From Home. U.S. Dept. Agr., Economic Res. Serv., Washington, D.C.

CHAPTER 5

The Feasibility Study

IMPORTANCE

The feasibility study is essentially an analysis of the market information, the operational concepts and the financial considerations that have been gathered for a particular project. The objective of the feasibility study is to determine whether the proposed project should be undertaken or abandoned. The decision is based on the economic factors involved. Owners or investors are not likely to commit funds for a project until enough information is gathered and analyzed to assure them of a reasonable rate of return. The data must indicate a fairly high probability of success.

The feasibility study identifies hidden factors or hazards that may not be readily seen by a cursory description of the project. Some reasons for abandoning a proposed food service project include inadequate financing, anticipated changes in the market, inadequate profit potential, poor location or excessive competition. Occasionally, the feasibility study will show areas where changes are needed to make the project acceptable to investors.

It is difficult to present a definite format for conducting the feasibility study because of the diversity of the types of food service projects that may be undertaken. Each feasibility study will reflect an analysis of the special requirements of the project under consideration. This indicates that some aspects of the feasibility study may involve greater research efforts in order to adequately guide the decisions that are to be made. For example, one type of project may require an in-depth analysis of the financing required, while for another project the marketing aspects may be more important. In any case, the data gathered and analyzed must be realistic so that the conclusions drawn from the study will be valid.

Each feasibility study has to be tailored to fit the project at hand. The suggested format and list of data requirements to be presented are generally applicable to most investigations of proposed new food service facilities. These items serve as a guide and in real practice the study is adapted to the requirements of the project under consideration. Feasibility studies are best conducted by professionals who specialize in this area. Many architects, food service consultants and accounting firms provide this service.

Before a feasibility study can be made, the analyst should be provided with some preliminary plans and have some information regarding the menu and prices that are proposed. The days and hours of operation are also required before a projection of total anticipated sales can be made. For general food service operations, the sales estimates are based on seating capacity, seat turnover and check averages. These data are usually obtained from the prospectus prepared for the project.

THE MARKET SURVEY

The market survey for the feasibility study may be accomplished for two different situations. In one case, a particular site may be under consideration for the proposed facility. In this situation, the market survey serves to characterize the immediate area of the site. In the other case, there may not be a particular site under consideration and market surveys of several localities may have to be made before deciding upon a site. In either case, the marketing data to be gathered are limited to the needs of the project. Only those areas of market information that relate directly to the demand for food service operations need be considered. Some of this information is obtained during the development of the prospectus. Additional market information required to complete the feasibility study is now gathered and summarized. The types of marketing data that may be gathered for a particular project are outlined in the categories shown below.

(1) Potential customers

location	ages
number	sex
types	occupations
income levels	spending habits

(2) Historical data

attractions	types of businesses
types of industries	climatological data

(3) Growth characteristics

population	transportation
bank deposits	labor force
telephones	government units
utility connections	taxes
building permits	recreation

(4) Competition

number and type of food	turnover rates
service facilities	sales volume
number of seats	quality of facilities
check averages	type of service

(5) Sales generators

conventions	residential developments
size	homes
types	apartments
facilities	shopping areas
lodging facilities	educational institutions
office buildings	recreational facilities

Sources

Marketing data for a particular locality may be obtained from many sources. A partial list of these sources and the data available are indicated.

Editor and Publisher. *Market Guide*, annual.

Market data for more than 1,500 American and Canadian cities. It covers location, transportation, population, households, banks, passenger automobiles, electric meters, gas meters, principal industries, climate, tap water, retailing and newspapers. Also provides population income estimates and retail sales for nine retail store groups by county and newspaper markets.

Hammond, C. S. and Co., *Hammond's Sales Planning Atlas of the U.S. and Canada.*

This is a series of maps and tables published in conjunction with Sales Management Magazine, showing county and city populations, retail sales and per household effective buying income.

Printers' Ink. *Executive's Guide to Marketing*, annual.

Surveys the total U.S. market, regional markets, special interest markets, business and industrial markets and international markets.

Rand McNally. *Commercial Atlas and Market Guide*, annual.

Market data include population estimates, characteristics, retail sales, bank deposits, automobile registrations, etc. for the principal cites in the U.S.

Sales Management. *Survey of Buying Power*, annual in the June issue.

Estimates of the population, effective buying income, total retail sales and sales of nine retail store groups for the U.S., states, counties and cities.

Sales Management. *Markets on the Move*, annual in the November issue.

Lists the number of plants and value added by manufacturers for regions and states. Also estimates population growth, effective buying income growth and estimated retail sales for areas.

Advertising Age. *Available Market Data*, annual in the May issue.

Provides a descriptive list of more than 1,900 items available from media, trade associations and other sources. The material is arranged in eight sections: national markets; farm markets; regional and local markets; distribution markets; professional markets; Canadian markets; and international markets.

U.S. Bureau of the Census. *Statistical Abstract of the United States*, and *Census of Business.*
    Provides typical census information and characteristics on population and businesses.

Institutional Food Service Manufacturers Assoc. 1969. *Bibliography of Food Service Market Studies and Related Source Materials.*
    A comprehensive bibliography of studies related to markets for food service operations.

Many local chambers of commerce maintain a supply of marketing data for their particular locality and are a good source of information.

SITE ANALYSIS

In the case where a particular site is to be evaluated for the proposed food service facility, considerable additional information is gathered and correlated with the market data. Because of the great variety and types of food service facilities, the site analysis has to be done specifically for the type of operation proposed. A site which may be ideal for a table-service operation may be very poor for other types of facilities. Chain operations have considerable background information on their customers and will try to find locations where they will attract the same type of customers.

Zoning

The best situation for a potential site is to have definite commitments on the use, restrictions and permits required for the proposed food service facility. Otherwise, considerable time and money can be expended in trying to change the zoning or in obtaining the necessary permits.

Area Economics

Data on the growth of business activity in the immediate vicinity of the site are gathered and evaluated. This may be done by types of businesses to get a feel of the direction of growth areas. A pattern of economic growth over several years is obviously preferred.

Competition

The evaluation of competition may be considered in two separate categories. Food service facilities that offer the same type of meals and service as the proposed facility will offer direct competition and are considered as a negative factor. Indirect competition includes food service facilities that offer a different menu and method of service. These may be a desirable factor since they are activity generators for a particular area. A lack of any type of competition near the proposed site should be carefully analyzed; it could mean a potentially excellent site or it could indicate a very poor site.

Information regarding existing food service facilities for a particular area can be obtained from travel guides, vacation guides and tour books.

Physical Characteristics

Top soil and subsoil conditions, slopes and surface drainage characteristics of a site are important from the standpoint of actual placement and construction of the building. Soil borings are desirable to determine the bearing capacity of the soil and to locate possible high water-table areas.

Facilities that will have to use septic tanks for waste disposal require percolation tests of the soil before county sanitarians will approve such systems.

Size and Shape

The potential site for the food service facility must be large enough to allow efficient placement of the building, parking areas, entrances and other exterior areas required. The preferred shape of the site for most facilities is square or rectangular. Triangular and other odd-shaped sites cannot be efficiently used unless they are very large. Possibilities of future expansion are considered when evaluating the size and shape of the site.

Land Costs

A potential site that has many desirable characteristics may have to be eliminated from contention because of excessive costs. Land costs, improvement costs and taxes are evaluated in light of the total project cost to make sure they are not out of line. This factor is evaluated in the financial part of the feasibility study.

Availability of Utilities

The availability or cost of obtaining gas, water, sanitary sewer, electricity, storm sewer and possibly steam at the proposed site are to be checked. Many urban locations present no problem; however, it may be quite costly to run utilities to remote locations.

The quality and capacity of the utilities should also be evaluated. Water quality is extremely important for food service facilities. Separate water treatment facilities may have to be provided in some instances.

Street Patterns

This factor is analyzed to determine whether street and traffic patterns tend to draw people to the site area or if they tend to diffuse the population as they travel to activity generators. Proposed new traffic routes or proposed changes in routes can be obtained from highway departments.

Positional Characteristics

The positional characteristics indicate the location of the site in relationship to activity generators. Distances and directions to shopping centers, commercial areas, recreational areas, etc., are evaluated. Activity generators that are several miles away from a site can still generate sales for certain types of food service facilities.

Traffic Information

Traffic information for streets surrounding the proposed site may be obtained from highway departments or local governmental agencies. If a traffic count has not been taken fairly recently or is not available, then sample counts may be taken at significant times during the day. Traffic counts are usually taken at noon-hours, weekend evenings, and Sundays. Counts taken over a period of several days should be used to eliminate biased results. Dinner-hour counts may be influenced heavily by commuter traffic and can be used for evaluating sites for take-home food facilities. They may not, however, be significant for other types of food service operations.

Visibility

The visibility of the site is evaluated by taking tours by auto or by foot from all directions. A good view of the facility is desirable even though signs are to be used for identification. This is most important for sites that are located on high speed routes that have heavy traffic.

Accessibility to the site and proposed parking areas should also be checked at the same time.

Services

Police and fire protection, garbage and trash pickup and other desired services are included in this factor. Availability, cost and quality of required services at the proposed site should be evaluated. This information can be obtained from city or municipal offices.

Availability of Local Labor

Considerations of the type of labor skills, ages and availability of personnel to staff the proposed facility are involved in this factor. Of special importance to the success of the facility is the availability of management talent that will be required to operate it. This factor is not usually critical except for remote or outlying areas.

These are some of the major factors involved in the early considerations of site selection for a new food service facility. Some analysts find a form such as the one illustrated in Table 5.1 a great help in gathering site information.

The techniques used in site analysis for food service operations are very changeable. It pays to be very careful for this part of the feasibility study since the future of the food service facility is largely affected by the site. The problem of correctly selecting a site can only be solved by an intuitive analysis of the key factors involved.

The experienced market and site analyst, in addition to collecting and analyzing the facts and figures, will personally tour the area within a reasonable radius of the site. He may also visit all nearby competitive facilities to get a better "feel" for the area. Interviews may also be a part of the analyst's procedure to see how local businessmen and potential clientele feel about the proposed food service facility.

FIG. 5.1. MANY CITIES HAVE RESTRICTIONS ON THE SIZE AND LOCATION OF SIGNS

TABLE 5.1

SITE ANALYSIS FORM

(1) Zoning
     Current zoning of site _____
     Use permits needed _____
     Height restrictions _____
     Front line set back _____
     Side yard requirements _____
     Back yard requirements _____
     Restrictions on signs (Fig. 5.1) _____
     Parking requirements _____
     Other restrictions _____
(2) Area Characteristics
     Type of neighborhood _____
     Type of businesses _____
     Growth pattern _____
     Proposed construction _____
     Other available sites _____
     Zoning of adjacent sites _____
(3) Competition
     Number of food facilities in drawing
        area of site _____
     Number of seats _____
     Type of menu offered _____
     Method of service _____
     Check averages _____
     Number of cocktail lounges _____
     Quality of drinks _____
     Bar service available at tables _____
     Annual sales _____
(4) Physical characteristics
     Type of top soil _____
     Type of subsoil _____
     Depth of water table _____
     Presence of rocks _____
     Load-bearing capacity _____
     Direction of slopes _____
     Surface drainage _____
     Percolation test results _____
     Natural landscaping _____
     Other features _____
(5) Size and Shape (Including sketch)
     Length _____
     Width _____
     Total square feet _____
     Square footage needed for building _____
     Square footage needed for parking _____
     Space for other requirements _____
(6) Costs
     Cost per front foot _____
     Cost per square foot _____
     Total cost of site _____
     Cost of comparable sites nearby _____
     Costs for land improvements _____

TABLE 5.1 (*Continued*)

Real estate taxes _____
Other taxes _____
(7) Utilities
Location, cost, and size or capacity of:
Storm sewer _____
Sanitary sewer _____
Gas lines _____
Water lines _____
Electricity _____
Steam _____
(8) Streets
Basic patterns _____
Width or lanes _____
Paved _____
Curbs and gutters _____
Sidewalks _____
Lighting _____
Public transportation _____
Grades _____
Hazards _____
(9) Positional Characteristics

	Distance	Driving Time
Distance and driving time to:		
Central business district	_____	_____
Industrial centers	_____	_____
Shopping centers	_____	_____
Residential areas	_____	_____
Recreational areas	_____	_____
Sporting events	_____	_____
Educational facilities	_____	_____
Special attractions	_____	_____
Other activity generators	_____	_____

(10) Traffic Information
Distance to nearest intersection _____
Traffic characteristics _____

Traffic counts:	Day	Time	Count
Site street	____	____	____
	____	____	____
	____	____	____
Adjacent streets	____	____	____
	____	____	____
	____	____	____

Anticipated changes _____
(11) Visibility
Distances of sight from:
Left _____
Right _____
Across _____
Obstructions _____
Location of signs _____
(12) Services
Quality of police protection _____
Quality of fire protection _____
Location of hydrant _____

TABLE 5.1 (*Continued*)

Availability of trash pick up	_____
Availability of garbage pick up	_____
Other services required	_____
(13) General Recommendations	
Suitability	_____
Desirability	_____
Other recommendations	_____

The market data and site analysis enables the analyst to advise the owner or investor in the following areas:

(1) seating capacity;
(2) most desirable type of service unit;
(3) expected seat turnover by days of the week and by months of the year;
(4) expected check average for each meal period;
(5) expected alcoholic beverage sales if a bar is to be included in the food facility.

The analysis of the market and site data is one of the points in the feasibility study where a decision to continue the project can be made. A keen analyst will recognize when the facts indicate a negative decision. If it appears at this point that the proposed project has insufficient potential for success, it must be terminated before additional funds are spent. If the data indicate a potential success for the project the feasibility study is continued.

COST ESTIMATES

After completion of the market study and selection of a site for the proposed facility, the financial aspects of the feasibility study are considered. Two important areas are evaluated. First, preliminary estimates must be made of the costs of land, building, equipment, furnishings and the amount of working capital needed. The second area deals with the projected income and expenses of the facility. These are usually prepared in the form of a tentative operating budget. Both these areas are of concern to the owner or investor because they indicate how soon he can expect to get his investment back and how much profit might be made. If the preliminary cost and profit estimates are not very encouraging, the owner should either modify the basic scheme of the project or abandon it completely.

Land and Construction Cost Estimates

The cost of land for the proposed facility can be obtained from realtors or by a real estate appraisal. The site development costs for excavating, removing rocks, and grading for driveways and parking areas are estimated by the architect.

The architect will prepare estimates of construction costs, including building equipment and utilities. These preliminary cost estimates can be made in different ways. One method, which is fast but may not be too accurate, is to use "rules of thumb" based on studies of actual costs of existing food service facilities. These costs are generally expressed in terms of the cost per seat. The cost per seat figures have to be used carefully because they can vary a great deal depending upon the size and style of facility involved. Typical cost per seat figures range from $1,000 to $3,000 or even higher, depending on the elaborateness of construction and furnishing.

Another method of obtaining preliminary cost estimates is to analyze costs of similar types of food service facilities that have recently been built. Most operators will willingly give out the costs they have incurred in building their facility.

Preliminary cost estimates may also be arrived at by using local construction costs per square foot or per cubic foot for similar types of buildings. Many construction contractors maintain up-to-date costs per square foot or per cubic foot of building space. The estimates should be obtained for approximately the same size building because size is an important variable of construction costs.

Regardless of the method used, the preliminary costs for maximum investment are needed in order to arrange the necessary financing.

Costs of Furnishings and Equipment

Cost estimates for furnishing and equipping the facility are determined by the interior designer and the food service consultant. These are estimates for equipment and furnishings in the kitchen, dining and public areas and do not include building equipment, such as heating and ventilating equipment. The building equipment costs are included in the construction estimates. The furnishings and equipment category does include items of office furniture, office machines, linen room equipment, and furniture for employee and guest areas.

Operating Equipment

The cost estimates for furnishings and equipment do not include operating equipment. Operating equipment encompasses such items as china, glassware, silverware, utensils, linens and uniforms. The cost estimate for operating equipment as shown in Fig. 5.2 is generally based on the starting inventories required of each of the items. These costs can be obtained from local suppliers.

FIG. 5.2. GLASSWARE FOR THE BAR IS CLASSIFIED AS OPERATING EQUIPMENT FOR ESTIMATING PURPOSES

Planning Costs

Estimates for planning costs have to be determined separately. Planning fees for members of the planning team can be estimated at 7 to 10% of the total construction costs, including equipment and furnishings. Land costs are not included when determining this estimate.

All these various cost estimates are added together to develop a figure for the total amount of money needed to build and equip the facility.

OPERATING CAPITAL

Operating capital refers to the money required to finance the food service operation after it opens until some inflow of cash begins. The money is needed for house funds, payments for supplies, payroll expenses and for other current bills as they become due. Operating capital requirements may be broken down into the following categories.

(1) *Cash on hand*. This is for the cashiers who will handle the cash transactions. The total amount needed will vary with the size of the operation and with the expected sales volume.

(2) *Cash on deposit*. Includes funds to meet current payrolls, utility bills, materials and supplies. The total amount on deposit will vary with the owner's desire to maintain a good financial position in meeting current obligations. Some funds for emergency expenditures should also be included.

(3) *Accounts receivable.* The increasing popularity of credit cards requires some money to handle the accounts receivable. This may be determined by estimating the volume of charge business anticipated and the time required to collect the accounts. Those operators who will handle cash sales only do not have to consider this category.

(4) *Inventories.* This category is to handle the beginning inventories of food, beverages and supplies. The food inventory may be estimated at 1% of the total annual food sales expected. Beverage inventories are frequently estimated at 5% of the expected annual beverage sales. Inventories of supplies vary with the type of operation; a rough estimate of 0.5 to 1% of annual sales can be used.

(5) *Prepaid expenses.* Prepaid expenses include such items as insurance premiums, licenses and interest payments. These may be estimated by contacting the appropriate agencies involved.

The accounts receivable and inventories are considered as current assets and are to be offset by the current liabilities in estimating the amount of working capital needed.

Current liabilities may be estimated for the following items. Accounts payable are usually on a monthly basis and any accounts can be estimated at one-twelfth of the annual cost of sales and services expected to be supplied by purveyors. Payroll and payroll taxes can be estimated for one week's time. The utility bills, local taxes, and other accrued expenses may be estimated at 1% of total sales volume. Any mortgage and other note obligations should also be included in the current liabilities category.

PROJECTED INCOME

The next step involved in the feasibility analysis is to determine the projected earnings for the food facility. A suggested format for estimating sales is shown in Table 5.2. Usually estimates for each of the

TABLE 5.2

FORMAT FOR ESTIMATING INCOME FOR THE PROPOSED FACILITY

Meal Period	Number of Seats	Estimated Turnover	Total Meals	Estimated Check Avg.	Estimated Daily Sales	Annual Operating Days	Estimated Annual Sales
Breakfast	___	___	___	___	___	___	___
Lunch	___	___	___	___	___	___	___
Dinner	___	___	___	___	___	___	___
Other	___	___	___	___	___	___	___
						Total	___

TABLE 5.3

ESTIMATED EXPENSES FOR FOOD SERVICE OPERATIONS

Cost of Sales	% of Total Sales	
Food	38	
Beverage	30	
Total food and beverage costs		36
Operating expenses		
Payroll	30	
Employee benefits	3.5	
Laundry	1.5	
China, glass, silver, utensils	2.5	
Utilities	3	
Supplies	2	
Advertising	2	
Insurance	1.5	
Licenses	0.5	
Telephone	0.3	
Administrative	3	
Miscellaneous expenses	0.2	
Total operating expenses		50
Total costs and expenses		86
Estimated profit before occupancy costs and income taxes		14

first three years of operation are made. This results in a more realistic estimate. Bar sales are usually estimated at 25% of food sales.

The expected annual expenses are also developed in a similar manner. Although many percentage figures are reported in publications for various categories of expenses, these should only be used as a guide. These expenses can vary widely from operation to operation. Table 5.3 identifies the typical expense items with suggested costs expressed as a percentage of total food and beverage sales.

The analysis of the projected earnings will determine whether or not the project is justified as conceived. If the proposed facility is deemed feasible, the planning process is continued by commissioning the planners. The planners are given the general requirements for the project as determined by the feasibility study. These requirements include total building size, number of seats and dining room square footage, number of parking spaces, bar space and any other space needed for special functions.

BIBLIOGRAPHY

ANON. 1965. The site and the menu: what makes a great location. Fast Food *64*, No. 6, 50–58.
CASE, D. R. 1968. Food service site selection. Cornell Hotel Restaurant Admin. Quart. *9*, No. 3, 21–24.

CELLA, F. R. 1968. Computer evaluation of restaurant sites. Cornell Hotel Restaurant Admin. Quart. *9*, No. 3, 25–37.
DARLEY/GOBAR ASSOCIATES. 1969. Restaurant site selection. Cornell Hotel Restaurant Admin. Quart. *10*, No. 3, 61–69.
DOWNS, A. 1969. Market trends in food service. Cornell Hotel Restaurant Admin. Quart. *10*, No. 1, 5–16.
ESPERSEN, H. W. 1966. The market-feasibility study in food facilities planning. Cornell Hotel Restaurant Admin. Quart. *11*, No. 1, 19–24.

CHAPTER 6

Planning of Functions

FUNCTIONS

The functional planning for the various areas of food service facilities may be accomplished in different ways. Experienced food service consultants have developed their own techniques of planning and can plan areas fairly rapidly. In order to develop the basic concepts of functional planning, a detailed presentation will be given. In actual practice, much of this planning is done in the designer's mind before any sketches or plans are developed and drawn.

The main concept of planning deals with functions. All food service facilities perform various functions in their day-to-day operation. General functions common to most operations include receiving, storage, preparation, production, service, warewashing and waste disposal. These functions can easily be related to the materials and products involved in the food facility. Other functions that are performed but are not easily related to materials or products include accounting, purchasing, management and communications. Typically, each function can be broken down into more specific items. For example, the general storage function may be subdivided into storage of meats, dry foods, beverages, linens, dishes, silver, and trash.

The first step in functional planning is to visualize all the necessary functions to be performed in the proposed food service facility. This obviously comes easily to experienced planners, but persons unfamiliar with planning may find it helpful to make a list of the functions. The more detailed the list, the easier the remaining steps of the planning process become.

Each function consists of a number of tasks. For example, the tasks involved in the preparation function may include weighing, cutting, mixing, blending, panning, moving and judging quality. These tasks vary from one facility to another depending upon the method of operation desired by the owner or manager.

The method of performing the tasks also depends on the type and form of materials involved, the kind of equipment to be used, the quality of finished products, and the skill of the persons involved. The evaluation and selection of these variables that affect the tasks are a part of the designer's responsibility. Hopefully, the best choice of materials, equipment and processes will be made, to facilitate performance of these tasks. Thus functional planning begins with identification of functions and visualization of the tasks to be performed for each function. A comprehensive list of tasks for food service operations is given in Appendix C. The tasks are listed by functional categories and may be used as a check list for this part of the planning process.

CONCEPTS OF FLOW

The identification and visualization of the functions and their associated tasks makes it easier to discuss the concepts of flow. Flow is identified as the movement of materials, workers, guests, equipment, forms or any other element involved in the operation of the food facility. The most important concept of flow, as related to planning, is to minimize the amount of movement required for efficient operation. As functions and tasks are visualized, planning

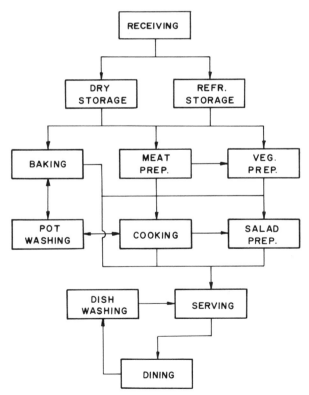

FIG. 6.1. A TYPICAL FLOW DIAGRAM FOR A FOOD
SERVICE FACILITY

for the methods of performing them should be guided by this concept of minimum movement.

There are many aids that can be used to plan the facility so that flow is minimized. The most common of these is the flow diagram. The flow diagram is developed by showing the flow of materials between the various functions that relate to a particular project. A simple flow diagram for food service operations is shown in Fig. 6.1. Flow diagrams show the flow of primary materials only. The functions shown on the diagram are connected by arrows that indicate the direction of flow. Different types of arrows may be used to identify the flow of different materials. The flow diagram aids the planner in physically locating the areas where the functions will ultimately be performed. The flow diagram does not have to be developed at this stage of the planning process, but may be done later when specific aspects of flow will be considered.

FUNCTIONAL REQUIREMENTS

Another reason for identifying the functions and tasks is to develop the various physical requirements needed to perform them. The basic requirements considered are equipment and space. For each function or task, the planner will determine the type of equipment to be used, and this in turn leads to the development of space requirements. The capacity of the equipment is not usually determined at this time because a careful analysis of the menu and scheduling are required. The determination of equipment capacity will be discussed in detail in Chapter 9.

In the development of equipment and space requirements, the planner has to decide how each of the tasks for a particular function is to be performed in terms of the materials and processes involved. To illustrate, consider the task of making a stew as one of the components of the cooking function. Some of the variations of the materials that may be used in making the stew are:

(1) entirely from fresh raw ingredients, both meat and vegetables;
(2) partially fresh vegetables and partially canned (i.e., fresh potatoes and others canned);
(3) partially fresh vegetables and partially frozen vegetables;
(4) all canned vegetables and fresh meat;
(5) all frozen vegetables and fresh meat;
(6) fully processed canned stew;
(7) fully processed frozen stew.

It can be seen that each of these variations in the ingredients will require different tasks and different processes for production. This in turn leads to different equipment types. The planner will evaluate the menu items to be produced and make the decisions regarding the type of production equipment to use. This same concept is used for all the other functions and tasks required to operate the facility.

Considerations of space requirements are also evaluated in a similar manner. The mere identification of the functions and tasks alerts the planner to the fact that some kind of space will be needed. The planner does not necessarily need to determine the final square footage of space now, but does consider whether a particular task requires floor space, work surface space and/or storage space. The designer is essentially developing the basic concepts for the operation of the facility. This is done prior to the planning of the actual physical areas. In other words, the planning of the operational methods is the key to the functional planning for the facility. A short discussion of some of these functional areas will illustrate and clarify the concept.

RECEIVING

The receiving function is very similar for most food service operations. The receiving of incoming foods, beverages and supplies is planned according to the types and volumes of different materials handled. The frequency of deliveries and the type of delivery service are considered for each type of material to be received. For large facilities, materials-handling systems may be utilized to simplify the movement of materials into and out of the receiving area. Many suppliers offer their products in palletized form, which simplifies the movement. The use of carts, trucks and conveyors will solve most materials-handling problems.

Planning of the materials-handling system for the receiving area is only a part of the total system for the entire facility, and the planner should consider all the various components of the handling system before making a final decision. Some may decide to use a single type of handling equipment for everything from the initial receiving to final service. Other planners may conceive a system which uses several types of equipment, each selected for its characteristics for handling certain types of materials. For example, mobile carts and trucks may be selected for handling food items, while conveyors may be chosen to handle dishes and other non-food items. The availability of a wide variety of materials-handling equipment enables the designer to develop many different systems.

Some temporary storage in the way of floor space and table space is required to check deliveries for quantity and quality. This space is designed on the basis of the larger amounts of frequently delivered materials. Additional space is planned for scales, storage of skids and hand trucks, and for other necessary equipment for the receiving function.

Consideration of waste disposal is also a factor in planning for the receiving function, since some partial trimming and cleaning of materials may be needed before they are placed in storage. Disposal of boxes, cartons and other packaging materials removed during the receiving function is also involved.

Architectural features, including the size and location of unloading docks and doors, may be developed at this time.

STORAGE

Planning for the storage function in food facilities includes dry storage, refrigerated storage, freezer storage, beverage storage and storage for non-food supplies.

Dry Storage

The dry storage function, like other storage functions, is necessary for on-the-site storage of frequently used materials. Storage requirements will depend upon the types of materials, frequency of delivery and the volume of each delivery. These variables are evaluated before functional planning of the storage area begins.

Dry storage areas for food items are planned to maintain temperatures between 50 and 70° F. The desired relative humidity is approximately 50%. For this reason, heat-generating equipment, such as motors and compressors, should not be planned for this area. Pipes carrying steam or hot water are insulated to minimize heat gain of the storage area. Protection against moisture from sweating cold water or refrigerant lines is also important. Planning for protection of the foodstuffs from insects and vermin is required for sanitary reasons.

Some space for storage of frequently used dry items can be provided in various work areas of the facility. This concept will reduce the amount of movement required to obtain the materials.

Refrigerated Storage

Refrigerated storage areas maintaining temperatures of 35° to to 40° F are required for fresh meats, vegetables and fruits, dairy products, beverages and for carry-over foods. Many planners are specifying smaller but more numerous reach-in refrigerators strategically located throughout the facility instead of one large walk-in storage. A combination of walk-in and reach-in refrigerators seems to be a good design for many types of food service facilities. The reach-ins are usually located adjacent to preparation and production equipment, or may be built-in under tables or counters.

The design of walk-in refrigerated storage areas is similar to the dry storage areas except for the refrigeration system required to maintain the desired temperature. The size and type of food service operation and the frequency and volume of deliveries will determine whether a walk-in refrigerated space is needed. It is thought that a walk-in refrigerator is feasible for operations serving over 300 to 400 meals per day. Reach-in refrigerators are generally designed to store for a shorter period of time and are ideal for smaller operations. Pass-through refrigeration units may be specified where their use will simplify the storage and movement of foods.

The increased use of frozen foods necessitates planning refrigerated space for thawing purposes. Requirements will depend on the volume and type of frozen foods to be used in the operation. Thawing space is generally designed to handle one day's production. Refrigerated space for finished items, including salads, desserts and appetizers, is planned accordingly.

Freezer Storage

Temperatures of -10 to -20°F are needed to safely store frozen foods. Designers are aware of the increased use of frozen foods that are partially or fully preprocessed, and plan accordingly. Some operations have gone almost exclusively to frozen foods. Freezers may be walk-in or reach-in, and requirements are dictated by several factors including the availability of seasonal items. The possibility of buying seasonal items in volume lots should be evaluated before the design of freezer storage is finalized.

Storage of Non-food Items

The design of storage areas for non-food items like dishes, glasses, flatware, utensils, paper goods, linen, cleaning supplies and furniture can take many different forms. They may be stored in rooms, on shelves, in cabinets or on specially designed racks. Figure 6.2 shows a utensil storage unit. In smaller operations, some items may be incorporated in the dry food storage area, but separate areas are best for larger operations. All chemicals, soaps, sanitizing compounds and other cleaning supplies should be stored separately because of their danger to foods. Separate areas are also desirable for cleaning equipment such as brooms, mops, pails, scrubbers and polishers.

In-process storage of items may be accomplished by special equipment such as self-leveling dispensers. The self-leveling dispensers shown in Fig. 6.3 are a very satisfactory method of providing storage for dishes.

FIG. 6.2. STORAGE FOR UTENSILS CAN BE PROVIDED BY SHELVING UNITS

FIG. 6.3. SELF LEVELING DISH DISPENSERS ARE IDEAL FOR CONVE-NIENT STORAGE

PREPARATION

The preparation functions for a food service facility are meat preparation, vegetable preparation, salad preparation and sandwich preparation. Specialty restaurants may have different or additional functions depending on their menu items. An example is the fish and shellfish preparation function for seafood operations. The various preparation functions are sometimes combined and performed in one area. Smaller facilities frequently combine the salad and sandwich preparation areas. Combined vegetable and salad preparation areas are also common.

Meat Preparation

The meat preparation function consists of cutting, chopping, grinding and portioning of meats and meat products to ready them for further processing. The meat preparation function has changed drastically over the years with the advent and increasing use of fully pre-portioned meats. Some operations may have minimal meat preparation areas where the only tasks involved are the opening of packages and the panning of the meats. Larger operations and commissary operations may still require a full meat preparation function.

The planning for the meat preparation function varies with the amount of preparation that will be done on the food service premises.

Vegetable Preparation

The vegetable preparation function historically involved preparing primarily fresh vegetables for cooking and salad production. Typical tasks associated with fresh vegetable preparation are trimming, peeling, washing, cutting and chopping. As with meat preparation, the vegetable preparation function can be minimized by utilizing various types of pre-processed vegetables. Canned and frozen items are generally used as alternatives to fresh vegetables.

Design and planning for the vegetable preparation function depends on the state of the raw materials and the subsequent tasks to be performed. Large operations choosing to use fresh vegetables will require the use of cutters, choppers, slicers, peelers and similar equipment. Type and capacity will be designed to handle the volume of vegetables to be prepared. Holding refrigerators are used if the preparation is done a day prior to usage.

Waste disposal is another aspect in planning for the vegetable preparation function. Mechanical waste disposal units are commonly used.

Salad Preparation

The function of salad preparation is that of combining and assembling ingredients prepared in the vegetable preparation area, or obtained from fruit and vegetable storage areas, into finished salads. Various quantities of meat, fish and dairy products are used in certain salads. The preparation of some appetizer items may also be a part of this functional area.

Design for the salad preparation function will depend upon the type and volume of salads to be produced. As indicated earlier, salad and vegetable preparation functions are frequently combined in smaller facilities. Another alternative is to combine the salad preparation with the sandwich preparation function.

Large food service operations, especially in the institutional field, will design for a separate mass production salad area as shown in Fig. 6.4. In this situation, assembly line concepts and related equipment can be utilized.

FIG. 6.4. MASS ASSEMBLY OF SALADS IS REQUIRED IN LARGE FOOD SERVICE OPERATIONS

The perishibility of salads necessitates planning of refrigerated holding facilities. Mobile refrigerated carts are selected by some designers as a method of transporting and holding the finished salads. Pass-through refrigerators are frequently specified for cafeteria operations.

Sandwich Preparation

The design of the area for sandwich preparation is based on the need for fast and efficient work methods. The work areas are planned to provide ample space for the ingredients used in the sandwiches, hand tools, and a normal flow of work. Custom-designed sandwich preparation areas are used for operations handling a large volume of sandwiches. In some cases the sandwich preparation area may be in a part of the serving area, as in cafeteria or counter-service operations. Assembly-line techniques and automatic wrapping machinery are typical designs found in institutional and in-plant feeding operations.

COOKING

The heart of all food service facilities is the main cooking function, and special care in planning for it is required. In addition to cooking all meat and vegetable items, the cooking area serves as the hub between the production and service functions. In many table-service operations, for example, the pick-up of food for serving is directly adjacent to the main cooking area.

The design of cooking areas varies from very limited facilities, as in fast-food and limited-menu operations, to the very extensive facilities of luxury table-service operations or in large institutional food services. In all cases, the design of cooking area is closely correlated with the various menu items to be processed. Considerations of cooked-to-order and batch cooking are important in arriving at the final design.

BAKING

Except in a relatively few cases, food service operations will not be involved in the production of a full line of baked goods. Even many large institutional operations in universities and hospitals confine their baking function to cakes, cookies and pastries, other items being obtained from commercial bakeries. Even the operations that do a good portion of their own baking will use basic mixes that simplify the tasks of the baking function. Full bakeries are occasionally planned for commissaries or central kitchens that supply several outlets. These may be planned to handle the conventional tasks of formulation, scaling, mixing, handling and makeup.

The advent of high-quality frozen pre-prepared unbaked goods that require only thawing and baking has also had an impact on the design of baking areas. Many of the pre-prepared items can be processed in the main cooking area, eliminating the need for a separate baking area completely. A study of the quality and availability of these items and their scheduling into the cooking area should be made before a final decision is reached. An economic analysis of the cost of full baking on the premises versus the use of pre-prepared baked goods may also influence the design of the baking system.

SERVING

The different ways of performing the serving function result in a variety of serving facilities that may be planned. Basic table-service operations require pick-up areas immediately adjacent to the cooking battery. Separate pick-up areas are used for salads, beverages and desserts. Some items, including rolls, bread, butter and water, are stored at waiter or waitress stations located in dining areas.

Serving-line facilities are planned for cafeterias, employee feeding and school or university feeding operations. Several configurations of serving lines can be used, depending on the total number of people to be served and the time allowed for serving. Straight-line configurations, as shown in Fig. 6.5, are the most basic and are characterized

FIG. 6.5. STRAIGHT LINE CAFETERIA COUNTERS GIVE A WELL DEFINED FLOW OF TRAFFIC

by easy access and well-defined traffic flow. The major problem with the straight-line configuration is its limited serving capacity per line.

Variations of the straight-line include the U-shaped counter and the herringbone design. These configurations give more linear space and increase serving-line capacity. The shopping center or scramble serving line system is characterized by an open square configuration of counters at the perimeters that allow traffic to flow freely in the center.   Total serving capacity of the shopping center or scramble system is much greater than that of the basic straightline configurations.

Other types of serving functions that may be planned are tray make-up conveyors for hospitals, cart assembly areas for banquets and room service facilities for hotels.   Each of these has special requirements and should be planned for efficient handling of the food to be served.

DISHWASHING

The dishwashing function is usually performed in a separate room or area which has to be well ventilated and illuminated, as shown in Fig. 6.6.   Acoustical tile and noise-absorbing materials are used to aid

FIG. 6.6.   DISHWASHING AREAS ARE PLANNED WITH SUFFICIENT SPACE FOR EASY HANDLING OF DINNERWARE

in lowering the high noise levels associated with this function. Modern dishwashing machines can be obtained to handle any volume of dinnerware.

Glass washing, which used to be a major problem in food facilities, is now better accomplished through the control of washing, rinsing and water additives.   In many cases it is possible to wash glasses satisfactorily if they are washed shortly after the water has been changed.   Other operators may prefer to have a separate glass washer.

Large hotel food service operations find it desirable to provide a separate silver room where silverware can be cleaned and burnished. The separate silver room provides a better means of control over the expensive silverware.

The design of the dishwashing area is dependent upon the total volume of dinnerware to be washed and the time required to accomplish the washing. Some operations may prefer to carry a large dinnerware inventory in order to spread the washing over a long period of time. This usually occurs between the meal periods. Others may decide to carry a minimum dinnerware inventory, and must therefore wash the items as soon as they are soiled so they can be returned to service immediately. Regardless of the system to be used, the designer will provide methods of sorting, soaking, washing and drying of the various dinnerware items. Appropriate handling and storage methods are also devised for both soiled and cleaned dinnerware.

POT AND PAN WASHING

The pot- and pan-washing function is also preferably done in a separate area instead of combining it with other areas as some small operations may be inclined to do. The basic pot- and pan-washing function can be handled with a three-compartment sink and sufficient space for storing the soiled utensils. A typical pot- and pan-washing area is shown in Fig. 6.7.

FIG. 6.7. A TYPICAL POT AND PAN WASHING AREA

In some operations, a large storage area for soiled utensils may be required because they are not washed as soon as they are received. This occurs when the same personnel who wash dishes also wash the pots and pans. Pot-washing machines are considered for large food facilities if they can be economically justified.

WASTE DISPOSAL

Every food service operation has different requirements for waste disposal and many factors should be evaluated before designing a system to handle this function: amount of waste generated, type of waste (paper, plastic, garbage, cans, etc.), cost of hauling and dumping, frequency of pickups, and stricter air and water pollution laws. In many cases, different systems for different types of waste will have to be designed. For example, incineration may be used for paper, disposal units for food wastes and a dumpster for cans, bottles and other trash.

OTHER REQUIREMENTS

The functional areas discussed can be easily related to space and equipment requirements because of their identification with the flow of materials. Other functional areas that should be considered may not necessarily involve material flow, but are important from the standpoint of total planning. These areas include facilities for guests and employees and special areas such as equipment rooms and maintenance rooms.

The functional planning for a food facility is completed when all the functions and their related tasks have been identified, and provisions for efficiently performing them have been outlined. The remaining steps of the planning process will be easier if the functional planning has been correctly and thoroughly accomplished.

BIBLIOGRAPHY

AVERY, A. C. 1967. Work design and food service systems. J. Am. Dietet. Assoc. 51, No. 2, 148–153

BANGS, O. E. 1968. A master plan for food service design. Kitchen Planning 5, No. 1, 19–21.

KAZARIAN, E. A. 1969. Work Analysis and Design for Hotels, Restaurants and Institutions. Avi Publishing Co., Westport, Conn.

KOTSCHEVAR, L. H., and TERRELL, M. E. 1961. Food Service Planning. John Wiley & Sons, New York.

SCHNEIDER, N. F., JAHN, E. A., and SMITH, A. Q. 1962. Commercial Kitchens. American Gas Assoc., New York.

CHAPTER 7

Planning the Atmosphere

ATMOSPHERE AND MOOD

The atmosphere of food service facilities is considered to be the total environment to which customers or users are exposed. Atmosphere is sometimes described as everything that makes an impression on people. It involves more than just the physical environment and decor created by the architect, food service consultant and interior designer. Contributing to the concept of atmosphere may be physical aspects such as unusual location, a spectacular view, the method of pouring a drink or a combination of interior colors, fabrics, spaces and textures, as well as such nonphysical aspects as the attitude of service personnel as exhibited in courtesy, ability, pleasantness and promptness. The architect, consultants and designers can develop the physical components of the atmosphere, but it is up to management to provide and maintain its non-physical components.

Mood is best described as the response of an individual to the various components that make up the atmosphere. Every individual experiences some type of reaction to the atmosphere that may be desirable or undesirable. If the individual response to the food service facility is favorable, the atmosphere has served to put him in a good mood.

Importance

Atmosphere has been identified as one of the inducements for people to dine out. Many people like to be in different surroundings to enjoy the dining experience. In addition to good food and courteous service, the diner is looking for a restaurant that offers luxury or excitement, or at least something pleasant. If a customer experiences a desirable dining atmosphere he is more likely to come back because of his remembrance of that experience. Atmosphere is one of the prime generators of repeat business and is an important aspect in the successful planning of food service facilities.

In the highly competitive commercial restaurant field, the planning of the atmosphere for new facilities is going to be more important. The coming generation of potential customers is growing up in an environment which associates dining out with more than just good food. They will be expecting to experience a variety of feelings, and these feelings will be a direct result of the atmosphere. The planning of atmosphere may well include specialized audio-visual equipment and other electronic devices to help create a particular mood.

Relating Atmosphere to the Customer

Many factors have to be taken into account when planning the atmosphere for a food facility, and they must be considered in light of the clientele who constitute the market. Just as food choice is a matter of individual preference, social custom, income level, needs of time, etc., the individual's choice of atmosphere is related to many of these same factors. People from varying backgrounds and engaged in different activities will seek out different dining atmospheres. The atmosphere has to be planned to appeal to the particular segment of the market that the food service facility wishes to attract. A well-planned restaurant is characterized by both the right menu offerings and the right atmosphere. The most efficiently planned production areas are of little use if there are no customers to serve.

Developing the Atmosphere

Among other things, the atmosphere to be developed for a food facility should attract attention, be pleasing to the eyes and provide an interesting change of pace. For example, an intimate, peaceful dining room provides welcome relief from noisy offices and industries. Likewise, a noisy cafeteria may actually be refreshing to students who are in quiet surroundings most of the day. The warmth and glow of a fireplace provides a welcome change in cold weather.

The development of the physical and psychological aspects of the atmosphere depends in great part upon the planners selected to design the facility. They must have a clear understanding with the owner of the particular needs and goals to be accomplished in developing the atmosphere. In addition to knowledge of the functional operation of the facility, the planners should be keenly aware of the type of clientele to be attracted. Only then can they come up with a suitable design that will be attractive as well as functional. It is then up to management to develop the non-physical aspects of the atmosphere to complete the total concept.

Perceptions of Atmosphere

Comfort is one of the key considerations in atmosphere planning. If individuals do not feel comfortable in their surroundings, the atmosphere has not been properly designed. Comfort is created when individuals feel secure and at ease. Security may be psychologically

FIG. 7.1. SOME INDIVIDUAL BOOTHS IN DINING AREAS PROVIDE SPACE FOR THOSE SEEKING PRIVACY

imposed by the use of red and orange colors and by privacy, which can be provided by booths and partitions. Figure 7.1 shows one way of using dividers to create private areas in the dining room. Dining rooms which have an expensive look may create feelings of insecurity because individuals feel status-conscious in such surroundings.

Atmosphere planning is dependent upon an understanding of the perceptual awareness of individuals as sensed through sight, touch, hearing, smell, temperature and movement. The primary considerations of these perceptions as related to a dining experience are summarized as follows.

Sight.—The perception of visual space involving lighting levels, colors, eye contact with fixtures and decorator items, and the use of mirrors and screens to expand or contract the visual space.

Touch.—Perception of seat comfort, body contact, and contact with floor, tables, tableware and upholstery fabrics.

Hearing.—Perception of noise levels of conversation, kitchen sounds, outside sounds, and music.

Smell.—Perception of cooking aromas, body odors, and material odors from fabrics such as linen and leather.

Temperature.—Perception of air temperature, relative humidity, body heat, cooking heat, radiant heat and heat of cooked foods.

Movement.—Perception of muscle activity required for access to tables and chairs, movement of servers and other customers, movement outside as viewed through windows.

It is important not to think of atmosphere as simply a combination of colors, lights and spaces, but how the individual is affected by those factors. It is the perceptual concepts that should be kept in mind when developing atmosphere. To clarify the concept of perceptual environment, consider the matter of space. A person's perception of space is measured more in terms of his freedom of movement than in terms of physical dimensions of feet and inches. A dining room one hundred feet long means very little to a diner. If he can walk across a smaller room without encountering obstacles, it will be perceptually large. On the other hand, if he must make his way around closely placed tables and chairs, it will be perceptually smaller. This is due to the feeling of crowding when his movement is restricted.

Temperature works in much the same way. It is measured in terms of contrast rather than by degrees on a thermometer. An individual just coming in from the cold will require less heat to perceive a feeling of warmth than someone who has been exposed to a heated room for a long time. The body heat of others is also an interrelated factor in how an individual perceives a crowded condition. Individuals who are in a cooler room may be seated closer together than those who are in a warmer room.

A person's eyes are probably the most important yet deceptive tools of measurement in perceiving feelings. The structure of the eye exaggerates activity or movement that takes place on the periphery of vision. Consequently, an individual can be in an uncrowded room, yet feel as if it is crowded if there is a great deal of action or movement around him. When obstructions are used to block out the activity or movement on the periphery of his vision, he will perceive the area as uncrowded.

Thus, individuals measure the atmosphere with their senses and evaluate it as desirable or undesirable. The atmosphere must be planned so that the individual's perceptions result in a feeling of comfort, ease and acceptability. With these concepts as a guide, the food facility planner should evaluate the many physical components of atmosphere that can be manipulated and arrive at a combination that will give the desired sensations. Table 7.1 identifies the physical components that affect the perception of atmosphere. Many of these components will be discussed in detail to show their relationships to the design of dining areas.

COLOR

Color is one of the visual aspects of the atmosphere as perceived by individuals; it is also one of the best tools that planners have to create a variety of moods. Most people make a number of choices based on color; they select their clothes, cars, houses, paints and even foods by color. Color can be used to induce a feeling of happiness,

TABLE 7.1

PHYSICAL COMPONENTS AFFECTING PERCEPTION
OF ATMOSPHERE

---

(1) Colors
(2) Illumination
(3) Noise
(4) Ambient temperature, relative humidity, odors
(5) Type of seating (tables, booths, counters)
(6) Furnishings; floor and wall coverings, drapes
(7) Table appointments; dishware, silverware, napkins
(8) Shape and size of rooms
(9) Layout of tables
(10) Appearance and dress of employees
(11) Menu design
(12) Sanitary conditions
(13) Exterior design
(14) Landscaping
(15) Age and dress of customers

---

to promote serenity or to stimulate hunger. It can attract people to one type of dining room and drive them out of others. Certain colors are especially important to the development of dining areas.

Effects on Individuals

Many experiments have shown that certain colors have a very strong emotional effect on most individuals. It is known that blue reduces excitability and therefore helps one to relax. Blue is also considered to be cooling, and is "easy" on the eyes. Green is a color that acts as a sedative. Yellow, on the other hand, is cheery, stimulating and attention-drawing. On dull, sunless days, people exhibit mental and physical sluggishness which is partially attributed to the absence of yellow, red and other stimulating colors. Red is associated with excitement and violence. Gray suggests coldness and is very depressing unless it is combined with livelier colors.

Color sensations can sometimes produce physical reactions that are not just of the visual system but affect the entire body. For example, persons exposed to predominately red colors exhibit increased blood pressure, quickened muscular reactions and greater emotions. Red also tends to produce restlessness and makes time seem to pass very slowly. In comparison, persons exposed to predominately blue and green colors have been found to exhibit slower muscle response and quicker mental and conversational response. Blues and greens also make time seem to go faster. Some of the common emotional responses caused by exposure to various colors are summarized in Table 7.2. These may be used to develop the type

TABLE 7.2

EMOTIONAL RESPONSES TO COLORS

Color	Effect
Red	Excites, stimulates
Orange	Exhilarates
Yellow	Stimulates, boosts morale
Green	Imparts serenity and tranquility
Blue	Lends liberation and leisure
Purple	Creates graciousness and elegance
Brown	Relaxes

of response desired in various areas of the food facility. The colors have to be predominant in an area and individuals must be exposed to them for a period of time.

Color Characteristics

Because of the strong effect colors may have on individuals, care should be taken in selecting them to achieve the desired result. One of the aspects of good color planning deals with contrast. A single predominant color, no matter how pleasing, cannot function alone. A restful green that is predominant would strain the part of the eye susceptible to it and eventually lead to eye and body fatigue. With a single predominant color individuals would have to look harder to distinguish objects because of the lack of contrast. Extreme contrast between very light and dark colors is also undesirable since they too result in eyestrain.

In general, the desired contrast can be obtained by using the following guides.

(1) Use a light color with a darker version of the same color. Pink and red result in a desirable contrast that is not fatiguing.
(2) Use a weak chroma of a color with a stronger chroma of the same color. A pale blue and a royal blue illustrate this combination of colors.
(3) Use a warm color with a cool color.
(4) Use complementary colors such as peach and gray-blue or pale pink and dull green.

Achieving the right amount of contrast along with maintaining the desired emotional responses is necessary to the creation of a pleasing environment for dining. Many of these colors recommendations can be used in other areas of the facility.

Color Classifications

Red, yellow and blue are the primary colors. They are referred to as primaries because other colors are derived from them. In their pure form the primary colors are too strong to use on large areas and therefore are used as accents.

The secondary colors are green, orange and violet and are mixtures of two of the primary colors. Green is obtained by mixing blue and yellow, orange by mixing red and yellow, and violet by mixing red and blue. Mixtures of primary colors and secondary colors result in the intermediate colors. Examples of intermediates are red-orange, yellow-green and blue-violet. The primary, secondary and intermediate colors are shown on a color wheel, as illustrated in Fig. 7.2.

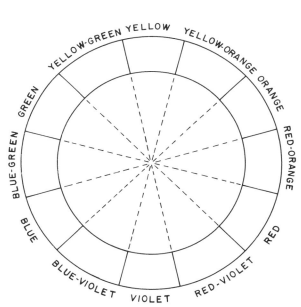

FIG. 7.2. THE COLOR WHEEL IS USED FOR IDENTIFY-ING PRIMARY, SECONDARY AND INTERMEDIATE COLORS

Colors are also classified as warm or cool. Red, orange and yellow are the warm colors; they seem to advance and convey a feeling of warmth. The cool colors are blue, green and violet; these are re-tracting colors and are cooling and relaxing. A combination of one warm color and one cool color results in the complementary colors used in color planning.

Color Harmonies

The problem of selecting colors that go well together or harmonize is solved by using one of five rules. These rules are related to harmonies and are identified as monochromatic, analogous, complementary, split complementary, and triad.

Monochromatic harmony uses a single color and is the simplest of color schemes. The single color can be expressed in the following ways.

(1) as the pure color itself;

(2) as a tint of the pure color (a tint is the pure color mixed with white);

(3) as a shade of the pure color (a shade is the pure color mixed with black);

(4) as a tone of the pure color (a tone is the pure color mixed with both black and white).

Analogous harmony is obtained by using any three or four consecutive colors on the color wheel. Examples of analogous harmony are red-orange, orange and yellow-orange; or red, red-orange, orange and yellow-orange.

Complementary harmony results by using any two colors that are directly opposite each other on the color wheel. Red and green, red-orange and blue-green, or yellow and violet are examples of complementary harmony.

Split complementary or near complementary harmony involves three colors. Any one of the two complementary colors and two colors adjacent to the omitted complementary color are used. On the color wheel, the split complementaries are in the form of a Y. Examples of split complementary colors are yellow, blue-violet and red-violet; green, red-orange and red-violet; and red, blue-green and yellow-green.

Triad harmony also involves three colors. These are selected by taking every fourth color on the color wheel. Two examples of triads are red, yellow and blue; and yellow-orange, red-violet and blue-green.

After a particular harmony is selected, then a decision regarding the tints, shades or tones of the colors is made. One or two of the colors selected will be used for the walls and other major surfaces. The other colors will be used as accents on smaller objects like drapes, table cloths and dinnerware.

The important points in color selection are as follows:

(1) Pure colors are usually too strong and brilliant when applied to large areas or surfaces.

(2) Colors should be selected under the same kind of lighting that

they will be used under. Colors selected under fluorescent lighting will appear different under incandescent lighting.

(3) Colors that are selected from a small sample will appear brighter when applied to large areas.

(4) Complementary, split complementary and triad harmonies always result in a combination of warm and cool colors. The desired atmosphere will dictate which color is to predominate.

(5) Black, white, brown and gold usually go well with any of the color harmonies.

(6) Texture is closely related to color application and usage is best considered at the same time the color choices are made.

Lighting and Color

As light modifies colors in many ways, the type of light source and systems of lighting should be considered when selecting colors. Pink lights, for example, have been shown to pale lipstick colors. Green lights have a tendency to show up wrinkles and should not be used in an atmosphere where a feeling of well-being is to be created. Another problem is the use of amber lights which tend to wash out colors. A well-chosen color scheme can be easily spoiled by poorly selected lights.

Lights and colors for work areas are quite different from those desirable for dining areas and should be planned separately.

Color Planning for Food Facilities

The uses of color in food service facilities are so numerous that space will not allow a complete presentation of all of them. Therefore, a guide to the uses of color is presented in Table 7.3. Note that many of the uses of color are related to other factors that affect an individual's perception of atmosphere.

The selection of colors is a very difficult task and one that requires skill, taste and experience. Color scheming does not end with the blending of wall colors with upholstery, fabrics and carpets, but includes the considerations of menus, dinnerware, uniforms and even the type of decorations. Just as the right colors can be used to make a food facility more attractive, the wrong colors can focus attention on features which should not be accented. Also, since color is so influenced by fashion and trend, these factors must be considered in the color scheme chosen.

LIGHTING

As mentioned previously, color and lighting are interrelated and it is difficult to discuss them separately. It is therefore important to

TABLE 7.3

GUIDE TO COLOR USAGE IN FOOD SERVICE FACILITIES

(1) The use of warm reds, browns, yellows, golds and oranges enhances the appearance of foods.
(2) Where emphasis is to be placed on fast service and high turnover, warm colors should dominate the major areas.
(3) Use colors in dining areas that are flattering to people. Colors that tend to make people look pale (green and grey) should be avoided.
(4) Use light colors in small areas to create the impression of size.
(5) Use warm colors in rooms that are windowless.
(6) High ceilings can be made to appear lower by using dark colors.
(7) Emphasizing horizontal lines by dark colors will make a ceiling appear lower.
(8) Low ceilings can be overcome by emphasizing vertical lines with dark colors.
(9) The end walls of long narrow rooms should be a warmer or deeper hue than the other walls to make them approach and make the room seem squarer.
(10) Undesirable features of a room can be painted the same color as their background so as not to emphasize them.
(11) Each room or area should have a mixture of warm and cool colors.
(12) Adjoining rooms or areas are best painted in harmonious colors.
(13) Avoid using too many different colors in one room or area.
(14) Use light colors to make objects appear larger if they are to be emphasized.
(15) Use dark colors to make rooms appear smaller.
(16) Use brilliant colors to bring attention to signs or other features.
(17) Dark-colored objects appear to be smaller than they really are.
(18) Maintain proper contrast to permit differentiation of objects from their backgrounds.
(19) Avoid highly reflective colors that tend to tire the eyes.

recall some of the fundamentals of color when thinking in terms of lighting. As with color, proper planning of lights can achieve dramatic effects and aid the creation of the desired atmosphere.

Both sexes enjoy a type of lighting which makes them look their best. This factor is of great importance in the planning and design of lights for dining areas, bars, restrooms and other public spaces.

The best system of lighting for restaurants appears to be a combination of indirect, direct and spot lights. These lights can be arranged to accomplish the desired flexibility required for the various meal periods. Areas should be well lit for breakfast and lunch, while less lighting is desired for evening meals. The installation of rheostats will provide this flexibility.

In considering the lighting system, the amount of daylight entering an area should be considered. Total glass area can be specified by the architect to adjust for this factor. The use of tinted glass may be considered for some situations.

Type of Lighting

The ultimate type of lighting for dining areas has traditionally been considered to be candlelight. The reddish flame of candlelight is flattering to people and to most foods. The flickering of the flame adds to the creation of a desirable atmosphere.

Alternatives to candlelight are incandescent and fluorescent lights. The economy of operation of fluorescent lights favors their installation in large areas. Incandescent lights would be the best choice in dining areas because of their red color enhancement. Properly selected fluorescent lights may also be used in dining areas if sufficient red tones are used in the color scheme. The deluxe warm white fluorescent tubes are the closest in color tint to incandescent bulbs and would be recommended.

Uses of Lights

As with color, lighting can do much toward creating atmosphere by correcting spacial deficiencies and accenting desirable areas. To illustrate, a low ceiling can be made to appear higher if it is well-lit; high ceilings will appear lower if they are dimly lit. Care should be taken not to light the long walls brightly in a narrow room since it will appear to be even narrower. Dark walls will show up better with bright lights, and if the color is to be accented, the illumination level has to be high. Bright lights are placed above normal eye levels to minimize glare. The same concept applies to candles since they too

FIG. 7.3. A WELL-LIGHTED SERVING COUNTER HELPS
INCREASE SERVING LINE RATES

can create glare. Candles may be placed in frosted globes if they are at eye level or slightly below.

In dining areas, it is best to concentrate illumination on the seats and tables and perhaps on special design features. The ceilings and walls should not be so brightly lit that they detract attention from the room.

Bright lights may be used to create a brisk atmosphere which, if service is fast, results in a high turnover of customers. Serving areas, as illustrated in Fig. 7.3, should be well-lighted. Some operations may use full lighting for a high turnover at lunch and then dim the lights for evening meals in hopes of attaining higher check averages.

Colored Lights

A popular design trend is to use various-colored lights for food service facilities. Careful selection of colored lights will enhance the total atmosphere. The first consideration is to coordinate the colored lights with other colored objects and color schemes used in the room. This is important, since certain colors will take on strange off-colors when subjected to colored lights. Red colors will appear very dark under blue or green lights and olive-green colors look brown under yellow lights.

Colored lights affect the appearance of the faces and clothes of people. Red lights have the advantage of flattering complexions and tend to enhance the color of fabrics. Red lights also have a good effect on most foods.

Green and blue lights are undesirable for illuminating areas where people will be present. These lights tend to distort the red hues and are unflattering because of this. Green and blue lights may be used for inanimate objects that serve as accent pieces.

The use of pink, ivory or amber lights is suggested for areas where skin tone is important, as they are warm and impart a friendly and inviting feeling. It is better to use tints of colors rather than strong hues.

Lighting Levels

Lighting should not only provide atmosphere but should reach a satisfactory level of illumination from a practical standpoint. If the lighting level is too high, individuals will have a feeling of exposure; or if too dim, they may feel fearful. For these reasons, there should be enough light so a person can see, yet not so much that he feels uneasy. One method of attaining such an arrangement is to lower the height of ceiling fixtures, as shown in Fig. 7.4. This provides a

FIG. 7.4. LOWERING CEILING FIXTURES ENABLES PEOPLE TO SEE THEIR FOOD WITHOUT SIGNIFI-CANTLY INCREASING THE GENERAL LIGHTING LEVEL

sufficient amount of light and at the same time results in a comfortable soft effect.

Food service lighting levels typically will range between 5 and 50 foot-candles; 30 to 50 foot-candles are used for breakfast and lunch. A level of 5 to 30 foot-candles, depending on the atmosphere, is used for evening meals. Public traffic areas and stairs as shown in Fig. 7.5, will require a minimum of 30 foot-candles.

FIG. 7.5. LIGHTING LEVEL AT STAIRWAYS IS IMPORTANT TO THE PREVENTION OF ACCIDENTS

The lighting level in all areas must be sufficient to make the other elements of the atmosphere visible. It is senseless to spend a great deal of time and money creating a striking color scheme and then ruin it with poor lighting. Any area with less than 5 foot-candles of illumination may as well be colorless.

Placement of Lights

The light most complimentary to human faces is from a source that is at eye level or slightly below. High light angles produce grotesque facial shadows by deepening eye sockets and showing every wrinkle and hollow in the skin. The traditional table lamp and table candles are recommended because their position as a light source is ideal. The light source should not be bright enough to cause glare.

One misconception about lighting is that it should be shadowless. In reality, the excitement of good lighting comes largely from its shadows and variations in brightness. Flat, shadowless lighting is dull and monotonous. The general lighting system for an area needs the accents of bright areas which come from direct light sources. These may take the form of wall brackets, chandeliers, downlights or spot lights. Recessed ceiling downlights of low intensity are very satisfactory for lighting dining areas. They emphasize the table areas and are very pleasant to the eyes.

ACOUSTICS, NOISE AND MUSIC

Other physical components of atmosphere are the level of noise and type of sounds present. The acoustical environment for the facility should be planned so the individual is not aware of noise. Aside from dinner music, sounds are to play a passive role and never attract attention. The design goal is to create a balance between quiet and noise. Many people are uncomfortable in a room which is very quiet. A noisy room creates tension and irritability. For dining rooms, a satisfactory acoustical environment has a reverberant sound level that is high enough to be heard, but not so high that individuals at nearby tables can distinguish what is being said.

Correct planning for the acoustical environment contributes to the development of the desired atmosphere. The sensitivities of individuals to various sounds require control of undesirable noise and maintenance of desirable sounds at an acceptable level.

Sound Characteristics

Sound may be considered to be a pressure wave and is compared to the ripples spreading out from a pebble dropped in water. If the sound is not restricted, it will spread out in all directions. The speed of sound in air is about 1,100 feet per second. Any sounds produced in open air will travel directly from the source to the listener. In a room, however, sound is reflected from the walls, floor and ceiling, and can build up a general sound level much greater than that which results from the same source in open space. Sounds that are repeatedly reflected become noise or unwanted sounds. Noise at a high enough level causes irritation and fatigue. It can interfere with communication and concentration and become very distracting and disturbing.

The intensity of sound is measured by the decibel. A sound intensity of one decibel is at the threshold of audibility for the normal human ear. A sound intensity of 20 decibels may be compared to a whisper. The normal speaking voice has an intensity of about 60 decibels. Any sound intensities over 100 decibels for any length of time are undesirable, and constant exposure can cause partial loss of hearing.

When there is a source of sound in a room, the level of noise at any position is made up of two parts. The first part is the direct sound traveling straight from the source to the position under consideration. The second part is the reverberant sound, which is the sound reaching the position after multiple reflection from the room surfaces. Fig. 7.6 illustrates these two different parts of sound.

The intensity of direct sound falls off as the distance from the source increases. Direct sound is reduced by about 6 decibels each time the distance from the source is doubled. Reverberant sound levels will generally be at a uniform intensity throughout the room.

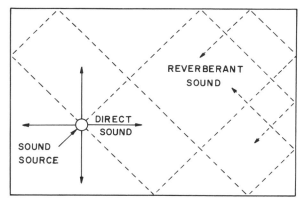

FIG. 7.6. DIRECT AND REVERBERANT SOUND IN A ROOM

Direct sounds are predominant at positions close to the source, while reverberant sounds will dominate positions remote from the source.

Noise Control

The problem of controlling noise levels is basically a matter of suppressing the sounds from the source and/or reducing the amount of reverberant sounds. Sound-absorbing materials are used to minimize both types of sounds. In some instances, the source of the sounds can be isolated by coverings or baffles. Kitchen areas are very difficult to sound-proof because of the materials used in the construction of the room and the large amount of metallic equipment present. Hard, dense materials, like quarry tile or clay tile used for kitchen floors and tiled wall surfaces, reflect a large portion of the sound striking them. Stainless steel surfaces actually act as sound surfaces much like a drum. In these areas, it is desirable to increase the amount of sound-absorbing materials as much as possible to overcome the severe noise problem.

In addition to acoustical treatment of walls and ceilings, carpeting where permitted will also help. Local sanitarians should be consulted before specifying carpet for production areas. The sound-proofing of metal surfaces by undercoating will reduce the noise created.

One method of handling noise problems in dining areas is to vary

FIG. 7.7. PARTIAL ISOLATION OF BAR AREAS WILL REDUCE NOISE LEVELS TO THE REMAINING DINING AREAS

the spacing of tables. The distance between diners at one table should be appreciably less than the distance to diners at adjoining tables. If a greater density of seating is desired, the use of screens or partial partitions will reduce the sound levels. Bar areas tend to be noisy and can be partially partitioned as shown in Fig. 7.7.

Music

The use of music as a desirable sound is one way of enhancing the audible environment. Music has a direct effect on the mood of individuals. Background music should be selected so it does not attract attention. It should be soft, inoffensive and as characterless as possible. The correct use of background music can put customers in a good mood for dining.

CLIMATE CONTROL

Climate is another facet of atmosphere planning that merits careful consideration. It is one of the important factors affecting the comfort of people. Most individuals are very sensitive to thermodynamic phenomena and variations from an ideal climate are easily noticed and quickly lead to discomfort. Customers will quickly respond to environmental conditions that are too hot, too cold, too drafty, too stuffy or too damp.

The ideal climate for dining consists of temperatures between 70 and 75° F with a relative humidity of 50%. Thermodynamic comfort is a function of activity and other factors such as age, sex and the amount of clothing worn. Needless to say, the climate should be designed for the particular type of patron that the facility is to be planned for. Higher-priced operations will usually attract people who are accustomed to slightly higher temperatures. Women prefer higher temperatures than men and children require less heat than both men and women. People who are in active occupations prefer lower temperatures.

The amount of clothing worn during the different seasons reflects the needs of different temperatures. People will be wearing lighter clothing in the summer; therefore, slightly warmer than normal temperatures would be appreciated. Clothing worn in the winter is heavier and temperatures should not be allowed to get too high. The effects of colors and lighting are evaluated before a particular temperature level is decided upon.

Temperature can be used to some extent to affect a desired turnover of customers. Many fast-food operations may want lower temperatures to keep the customers on the move and thereby increase the turnover rate. The opposite is true in more luxurious dining rooms where turnover is not stressed. Customers are inclined to be more relaxed in a higher temperature, and the warmth is conducive to a leisurely meal of several courses. The ideal design is to have a system where the temperature can be precisely adjusted for the particular situation.

Climate control in most regions requires both heating and air conditioning. The systems should have sufficient capacity to maintain the desired temperature and relative humidity. Air inlets and outlets should be placed to avoid drafts.

Odors

Climate control also includes the control of odors. Odors are an important part of the atmosphere, because smell usually evokes much deeper memories in individuals than either vision or sound. People are often uncomfortable in odor-free surroundings, and pleasant odors can attribute to the desired atmosphere. The popularity of display cooking areas in the dining room is partially caused by the cooking aromas that are emitted.

Odors have to be controlled or they will blend and can become quite offensive. This is very noticeable in dining areas where the air circulation system may bring in varied kitchen odors. Mixing the odors of fish and steak, for example, is not at all appealing to the person eating the steak. This is very disturbing to individuals because taste is largely a matter of smell. If the odors cannot be controlled and separated, or if they are undesirable, they should not be allowed to seep into the dining room. One method of accomplishing this is to maintain the air pressure in the dining room at a higher level than the air pressure in the kitchen.

FURNISHINGS

Furnishings for the dining area are also correlated to the type of atmosphere to be planned. The first thing that an individual does upon entering a dining room is to look for a place to sit. Therefore, arrangement of tables, chairs and auxiliary furnishings does much to affect the initial impression of customers. Many people do not like to sit at exposed tables because they feel observed. This problem is overcome by the use of booths or by planters that act as partitions. Changes in elevation, as illustrated in Fig. 7.8, can also be planned to break up large exposed areas.

Tables and Chairs

Tables, chairs and banquettes should be large enough to seat diners comfortably without crowding. Distances between tables are sized to

FIG. 7.8. LARGE AREAS CAN BE BROKEN UP BY
CHANGES IN ELEVATION

enable waiters or waitresses to move through the area while serving
and allow diners to eat and converse without being distracted.

Selection of chairs is critical since the greatest body contact is
made with them. Chairs must have suitable shape, angle of seat and
back, size, relationsihp to table, and tactile qualities to be comfortable. The chairs shown in Fig. 7.9 are suited for luxurious dining.
The essential dimensions for comfortable chairs are shown in Fig.
7.10.

Table space of at least 26 in. should be allowed for chairs without

FIG. 7.9. COMFORTABLE CHAIRS AND TABLES CONTRIBUTE TO A PLEASANT
DINING ATMOSPHERE

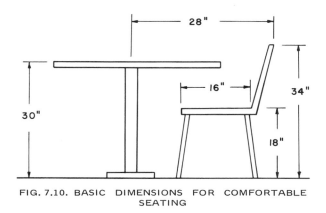

FIG. 7.10. BASIC DIMENSIONS FOR COMFORTABLE
SEATING

arms to provide elbow room. Armchairs require a minimum table space of 28 in. for comfort. The preferred height of chair seats is 17 to 18 in. for adults. A minimum of 12 in. of space is needed between the top of the chair and the bottom of the table.

Drapes and Fabrics

The selection of drapes, carpeting and fabrics is guided by the need for variations in textures, colors and shapes. These materials may be chosen to blend with or contrast with the architectural features of the building.

Drapes and floor coverings are selected to give an overall appearance of unity and balance. Various fabrics are selected to add warmth and coziness to a room and to relieve any monotony in the shape of the room. Fabrics contribute not only by their visual impact, but by the fact that they are more pleasant to touch than hard surfaces. Designers may use grass wallpapers, ceramic tile, cork, linen, silk, brick and other materials that are textured and appealing for wall coverings. Carpeting adds a feeling of intimacy and comfort because it is a point of contact.

Pictures

Pictures and prints used to decorate wall areas add considerably to the atmosphere. An advantage in using these items is that they can be easily changed. The pictures selected should not clash with the decorative scheme. The shape and size are correlated to the walls on which they will be placed. Colors within the pictures or on frames should blend with the overall scheme of the room to give a coordinated appearance.

Table Settings

Table settings can enhance the appeal of the dining atmosphere. Customers notice the tableware they are using and will thus form an impression of the restaurant. Each item placed on the table is selected to add to the feeling and mood to be created in the room. This pertains to dishes, glasses, silver, napkins and tablecloths.

EXTERIOR DESIGN

The term exterior, as used in food facilities design, is taken to include signs, landscaping, parking areas, building structure, doors and windows. The objective of exterior design is to attract customers. To perform this function effectively, the exterior must convey the correct impression of the type of food facility into which the customer is being invited. Exterior design, as illustrated in Fig. 7.11, has to be coordinated with interior design to provide the total atmosphere.

Visibility

One problem to be dealt with in exterior design is the matter of attracting initial attention. This is a problem of visibility as seen through the eyes of pedestrians and people in slow- or fast-moving cars. An attractive sign, large enough for the situation, is generally accepted as the best method of attracting attention. The placement of the sign must ensure that drivers are aware of the facility before it appears in view. In some locations, signs may have to be placed at considerable distances from the building. The most effective signs are those that are short and to the point.

Attraction is also gained by the exterior treatment of the building. This includes the size, shape, colors and materials used in construction. The first impression of an interior of a facility is gained from the exterior. This impression is derived not solely by the exterior design but from glimpses of the interior that are provided by windows. Windows are so located as to frame the parts of the interior that they expose.

Exterior Color and Lighting

The aspects of color and lighting were discussed earlier in connection with creating the interior atmosphere. They have as great an importance in the design of the exterior of the facility. Color and lights can be used in signs, facades, building elements and landscaping.

Color usage on the exterior can follow the same general guidelines presented for interior use. An additional consideration is to let any

FIG. 7.11. DESIGN OF EXTERIOR AREAS HAS TO BE COORDINATED WITH THE INTERIOR DESIGN OF THE FOOD FACILITY

natural landscaping provide much of the color. In this case, the building elements can be finished as plainly as possible so as not to compete.

Floodlighting is frequently used with success when the architectural features of the exterior are appealing or dramatic. Care must be used in sizing and placing windows in floodlighted areas to prevent glare into the building.

Decorative Detail

The amount and kind of decorative detail used on the building exterior is chosen to reflect the total atmosphere concept of the food service facility. Some designers may prefer to rely on the elegance of simplicity and use little, if any, decorative detailing. On the other hand, facilities with perhaps a national theme may require carefully selected exterior details to complete the concept of total atmosphere.

Entrances

The entrance door to the facility can form the climax of the exterior attractiveness. It should be selected in accord with the overall design of the building exterior. Doors may be all glass, half glass, wood, metal, plain or with panels. Separate entrances to the bar are provided if the bar will be used by non-diners. Entrance doors are located for easy access from streets or parking areas.

Whether to provide an entrance area or not is largely a matter of choice. An entrance area can have several desirable functions: it can convey a sense of spaciousness and enhance the atmosphere. Entrance areas also provide a meeting place for people and can be used as waiting space during rush hours.

Landscaping

Although maintenance of landscaped areas is costlier than of blacktop or gravel, a well-landscaped exterior may overcome the added cost by attracting more customers. Landscaping provides the setting for the facility. Another use of landscaping is to hide undesirable service areas or views from dining areas that are not pleasant.

The landscape architect may use contours, plant textures, heights, rocks, pathway surfaces or garden furniture to achieve the desired exterior appearance. In laying out the landscape, important views are selected and foregrounds and backgrounds are developed for them. The landscaping must harmonize with the exterior features of the building so that a good impression is created from all angles of view.

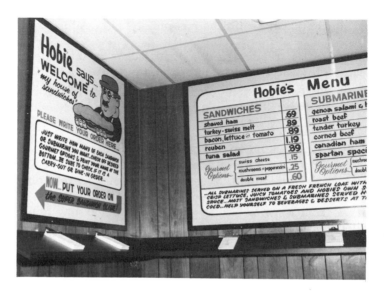

FIG. 7.12. DESIGN OF DISPLAY MENUS IS A PART OF PLANNING
THE ATMOSPHERE

PERSONNEL

The atmosphere for food service facilities is created for people who want to be satisfied by that environment. In the long run, people will be more influenced by the employees that they come in contact with than by anything else. The importance of retaining good employees and keeping them in a pleasant mood can not be underestimated as a vital part of the atmosphere. A cold welcome, poor service or indifferent attitude can ruin all the friendliness which the color, lighting, decor and furnishings have created. These physical components of the atmosphere are ineffective unless they are complemented by the human components.

The projection of atmosphere is carried to the point of selecting uniforms for waitresses, bartenders, bus boys and other personnel. The style and colors of uniforms are an integral part of the decor and add a touch of personality.

ADVERTISING AND PUBLIC RELATIONS

The atmosphere created for a facility is reflected by its name, the advertising, public relations efforts, brochures, signs and menus. Choosing a name is important to promotional materials to be used. The name and design concepts should be interrelated. The best names to use are those that are simple, easy to remember, easy to spell and pronounce, and are distinctive and reflective of the character of the food facility. The name will logically be the main feature in advertising and public relations.

The importance of menu design as a component of the atmosphere is frequently overlooked. The menu is the silent salesman for the restaurant and is designed to reflect many aspects of atmosphere. The descriptions of foods, lettering style, arrangement, colors, materials and size are involved in menu design. The design of display menus as shown in Fig. 7.12 is a part of the development of the atmosphere.

The design of the atmosphere for a successful restaurant is a very complex problem involving many factors. The additional efforts taken to develop the right atmosphere are justified by customer reaction and acceptance of the facility.

BIBLIOGRAPHY

ADLER, J., and ATKIN, W. W. 1960. Interiors Book of Restaurants. Whitney Publications, New York.
BISHOP, M. L. 1966. Atmosphere for gourmets. Interiors 125, No. 8, 125–127.

HALSE, A. O. 1968. The Use of Color in Interiors. McGraw-Hill Book Co., New York.
MOTTO, M. 1970. Profit by design. Cornell Hotel Restaurant Admin. Quart. *11*, No. 1, 113–117.
NEWELL M. 1965. Mood and Atmosphere in Restaurants. Barrie & Rockiff, London.

CHAPTER 8

Workplace Design

DEVELOPING WORKPLACES

One of the steps in planning a food service facility for maximum efficiency and productivity is the design of the workplaces. Workplaces are identified as the location and facilities where one or more employees can perform their respective tasks. The design of workplaces includes determining the necessary floor space, work surface space (see Fig. 8.1), storage space and necessary equipment. As emphasized earlier, identification of the tasks that must be accomplished is one of the first steps in planning a restaurant. At this point in the planning process, a further evaluation of the tasks is needed. Decisions regarding the specific materials required and the work methods to be used are finalized. Questions to be resolved include the following.

(1) Who will do the task?
(2) Will the task be done manually?
(3) Where will the task be done?
(4) What are the form, shape and characteristics of the materials?
(5) What hand tools will be required?
(6) What kinds of utensils will be used?
(7) What type of equipment is needed?
(8) What is the best work pattern to use?
(9) How will the materials be brought to and removed from the workplace?
(10) What must be stored at the workplace?

One method of systematically deciding some of these questions is by a detailed analysis of the menu. This involves taking a typical menu and evaluating each of the items listed. The menu analysis may be done by using the format illustrated in Table 8.1. The use of standard recipes for each menu item is very helpful in completing this analysis.

The menu analysis will identify the workplaces needed to produce the food items only. Workplaces for processing non-food items are developed by a similar analysis of the tasks required for processing the various items. This will enable the planner to develop workplaces for dishwashing, pot and pan washing, linen sorting, and can washing, to name a few. Similarly, the processing of paperwork will lead to

113

FIG. 8.1. WORK SURFACE SPACE FOR CERTAIN TASKS INVOLVED IN BAKING REQUIRES SPECIAL DESIGN

the development of workplaces for purchasing, inventorying, personnel management, and cost control tasks.

Having accumulated the desired information, the designer will develop the workplaces by providing for the following areas:

(1) Adequate floor space for the worker to move around in.

(2) Working surface space for the task; this may take the form of a work table, a counter surface or in some cases a piece of equipment used for working surface space.

(3) Space for temporary storage of incoming materials. Incoming materials may be placed on tables, carts, in tote pans or on specially designed equipment. Soiled dish tables are illustrative of the type of space needed.

(4) Space for temporary storage of finished products. Examples of this type of storage are salad carts, hot food-holding equipment, mobile shelf units, and even conveyors. A mobile cart

TABLE 8.1

MENU ANALYSIS FOR WORKPLACE DESIGN

Menu Item	Portion Size	Total Portions	Matls. Req'd.	Process Req'd.	Utensils Needed	Hand Tools	Work Surface	Equip. Req'd.
1.								
2.								
3.								

FIG. 8.2. MOBILE TRAY CARTS PROVIDE STORAGE
FOR FINISHED FOOD PRODUCTS

for holding trays of salads as shown in Fig. 8.2 is a versatile
piece of equipment.

(5) Space for storage of frequently used minor materials and ingredients. Seasonings, condiments, dressings and sauces may
be stored in special containers at the workplace.

(6) Space for hand tools required for the task.

(7) Space for the floor-mounted or free-standing equipment required for processing.

A brief description with recommendations for designing the workplaces for general food service operations will be given. Different designs may have to be developed for special operations that have special
requirements.

Floor Space

The floor space required for a worker to accomplish manual tasks is frequently referred to as work aisle space. Work aisles are separated from traffic aisles as much as possible to assure minimum interference with the worker. The amount of space required for a single-person work aisle varies from 24 to 36 in. A 24-in. work aisle is the bare minimum and would not be suitable for tasks that require bending and stooping, or where equipment components like doors and controls extend into the aisle. A 30-in. work aisle is desirable, since this allows freedom of movement for the worker. When oven or steamer doors extend into the aisle space, additional room is alloted as needed for the situation.

For situations where two workers will be working back-to-back, the recommended minimum work aisle space is 42 in. This figure does not include the allowance for equipment projections into the aisle space. In most cases, an allowance of 6 to 12 in. is sufficient.

Work Surface Space

Requirements for work surface space are dependent upon the materials used and the types of hand and arm actions needed to work on the materials. The workers' hand and arm movements should be confined to the normal and maximum work areas as much as possible. The normal work area for a work surface is defined as the space enclosed within the arc scribed by pivoting the forearm in a horizontal plane at the elbow. The worker should be in a typical working stance. The arc scribed on the working surface will have a radius of 14 to 16 in. for most people. The area within the arc scribed by each hand describes the normal work area for each hand. Where the arcs overlap in front of the body is the normal work area

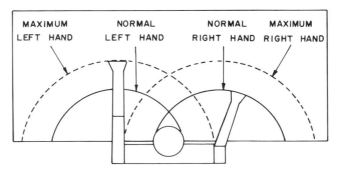

FIG. 8.3. NORMAL AND MAXIMUM WORK AREAS FOR THE
HORIZONTAL PLANE

for two-handed tasks. Hand actions for such tasks as cutting, slicing, mixing or assembling are best performed within the normal work area.

The maximum work area is defined in a similar manner except that the entire arm is pivoted at the shoulder. Figure 8.3 illustrates the normal and maximum work areas in the horizontal plane. Locations outside the maximum work area require bending of the body to reach them and therefore movements to these locations should be kept to a minimum.

In consideration of the normal and maximum work areas, the work surface for most tasks performed in food facilities can be done within a space 2 ft deep and 4 ft in width.

Height

The height of the work surface will vary with the type of task. Tasks involving small, light-weight materials can be easily done at a surface height which is about 2 in. below the height of the worker's elbow. The makeshift work surface shown in Fig. 8.4 is too low for comfortable work.

As the materials involved in the task become larger or heavier, the height of the work surface can be lowered. The lowest workable surface is at the point where the wrist bends when the arms are extended at the worker's sides. This height allows workers to use their shoulder and back muscles in handling the heavier materials.

FIG. 8.4. WORK SURFACES THAT ARE TOO LOW WILL LEAD TO BACK MUSCLE TENSION AND FATIGUE

General recommendations for work surface heights for light tasks are 37 to 39 in. for women and 39 to 41 in. for men. Work surfaces for heavy tasks are usually 34 to 36 in. high. Adjustable work-surface heights to fit both worker and task are the ideal design; however, an adjustable chair may be used to give the needed adjustment at lower cost.

Material, Tool and Utensil Storage

The materials, tools and utensils frequently used for tasks may be located in various places at the workplace. Overshelves, undershelves, bins, drawers and cabinets can all be incorporated into the design. The ideal location for storage facilities at workplaces is between waist and shoulder height. Items that have to be stored below waist level can be put on pull-out or swing-out shelving. Cabinets with fixed shelves below waist level are not easy to use. For the same reason, shelves and cabinets are not placed more than 6 ft above the floor. Self-closing cabinet doors and drawers are desirable. Mobile bins or carts may be used adjacent to the workplace if additional storage is needed.

A definite fixed location for all materials and tools to be stored at the workplace is good design. The locations are selected in accordance with easy work patterns and help employees to develop good work methods. Designers can often dictate a particular pattern of desirable motions and actions by their strategic placement of materials and tools at the workplace.

Mounted Equipment

Equipment that is to be mounted at a workplace should also be designed with the worker in mind. Slicers, mixers, kettles, grinders and similar equipment may be mounted on tables or carts at a height that will make them easy to use. Feeding and working height is important from the standpoint of safety. If the feeding or working level is too high, as illustrated by the kettle shown in Fig. 8.5, the worker will be forced to use awkward motions that can be hazardous.

Built-in sinks are required at many workplaces and should be placed at convenient heights. Sinks that are placed too low will require bending, and sinks placed too high are different to use. Preparation sinks used for light work are designed so the bottom of the sink is 10 to 12 in. below the worker's elbow. Sinks for heavier tasks, such as pot and pan washing, generally require a bottom depth of 16 to 18 in. below elbow height. As with other components of the workplace, sink heights should be designed to fit the worker and the task.

FIG. 8.5. THIS BENCH MOUNTED STEAM JACKETED KETTLE IS TOO HIGH FOR EASE OF USE AND CONVENIENCE

Free-standing Equipment

The use of larger pieces of food service equipment that will be free-standing or mounted to the floor deserve special attention. Some equipment, ranges and griddles, for example, can be considered as a separate workplace for certain types of cooking tasks. In other cases, additional work surface space may be required, and the combination of the equipment and a work table are considered as the workplace. Other combinations of equipment can be developed to meet the requirements of the tasks to be performed. The description of a workplace for one food facility does not necessarily apply to all facilities. An oven may be described as a separate workplace for a larger operation yet may only be one component of a workplace for another operation. The planner designs workplaces for the project at hand, which usually results in different combinations of equipment and work surfaces.

Regardless of the type and number of major items of equipment in the work area, the recommendations related to height and ease of use apply. Ranges, for example, may be set down into the floor so that pots placed on top of them are low enough to see into and stir easily. Similar recommendations apply to free-standing kettles, ovens, griddles, fryers, broilers and other items of preparation and production equipment.

Workplace Seating

Chairs are desirable at workplaces where the tasks require only hand and arm movements and are repetitive in nature. Seat heights between 24 and 30 in. will be suitable for most variations of workers and tasks. Adjustable foot rests are recommended so that leg circulation in shorter people will not be impaired when their legs dangle without support. Wherever chairs are to be used, the tables are designed to allow sufficient space for positioning the legs and feet. A minimum of 25 in. of clearance under the table is recommended.

After all the components of the workplace have been determined, they are arranged into a final design based on a normal flow of work. Symmetry in arranging the components of the workplace is important in conveying a sense of order. Most workers respond extremely well to an orderly environment and will work more productively under these conditions.

WORKPLACE ENVIRONMENT

The design of the environment where workers will perform their tasks is just as important as providing them with the required space, tools and equipment. Although certain tasks may require special environmental conditions, most workplaces are designed for the maximum performance of the worker. The concepts of environmental design are drawn from the field of human engineering. In the broadest sense, human engineering deals with the design of human tasks and the working environment that maximizes a worker's output with the least amount of input. Of the many areas encompassed by the field of human engineering, only those that pertain to the design of work environment will be highlighted.

Many of the factors affecting the environment were discussed earlier in relation to development of the dining atmosphere. These factors are now presented in the light of a worker's requirements. The differences between a dining and working environment are caused by the different objectives involved. There are, of course, several similarities in both environments.

Thermal Comfort

A worker is very aware of the factors that influence his sense of thermal comfort. Continuous exposure to high temperatures, high relative humidities and radiation effects from hot equipment cause most of the feelings of discomfort. Most workers perform best when these factors are within a fairly limited range of values. For example, effective temperatures between 65 and 70°F in winter and 69 to 73°F in summer are recommended for most tasks. These recommendations may be modified somewhat depending on the age and sex of the workers. Older people, especially women, prefer slightly higher temperatures. Some people can adjust to temperatures outside the recommended range without too much difficulty.

Relative humidity recommendations call for a range of 40 to 60%. Higher humidities cause thermal discomfort, and lower humidities result in the drying of skin and nasal passages.

Radiation effects result when a worker is exposed to extremely hot or cold surfaces even though the air temperature around the body is at a comfortable level. Working near ovens, broilers, fryers and other high-temperature equipment illustrates this effect. Continued exposure to high-temperature surfaces causes increased body and skin temperature that leads to thermal discomfort. Exposure to extremely cold surfaces results in heat loss from the body which produces the sensation of coldness.

Control of the worker's thermal environment is basically incorporated into the heating, cooling and ventilating system of the building. Special consideration has to be given to kitchen areas because of the large number of heat- and moisture-producing pieces of equipment present. The amount of heat and moisture added to the kitchen environment from equipment can be minimized by selecting equipment that is well-insulated or by specifying additional insulation. All pipes carrying steam or hot water to equipment should also be insulated. Proper venting of equipment is important, especially for mechanical dishwashers.

Lighting

Lighting recommendations for workplaces are determined by the amount of visual effort needed to accomplish a particular task. Obviously, tasks requiring greater visual effort, as reading or bookwork, will require a higher lighting level. The recommended lighting level for general areas of a kitchen that are non-work areas is 15 to 20 foot-candles. Working surfaces require 30 to 40 foot-candles for most tasks. Tasks that involve reading and working with figures should have a minimum of 50 foot-candles.

Either incandescent or color-improved fluorescent lamps may be used for work areas. General white fluorescent lamps are not desirable because of poor color perception that results with many foods. Incandescent lamps are available in a variety of types and permit flexibility of design. Fluorescent lighting systems are more expensive to install but operate more efficiently than incandescent systems.

Special care is required in planning the lighting system for workplaces to eliminate both direct and reflected glare. Direct glare is the result of locating the luminaire near the line of sight. Any luminaire that is placed within 30 degrees above the line of sight of the worker should be screened. Reflected glare occurs when highly polished surfaces in the line of vision reflect the light striking them. Stainless-steel tables and equipment, being especially good reflectors, cause many of the glare problems in food service facilities. Glare is highly disturbing to workers and leads to discomfort and fatigue.

Brightness ratios between the work and adjacent areas are considered in the design of the lighting system. Current lighting practice indicates that best results are obtained when the brightness ratio does not exceed 3 to 1, the work itself being the brighter.

A well-planned lighting system for workplaces should provide enough brightness for the worker to see everything he must see to perform his task efficiently. This includes light for seeing into drawers, shelves, cabinets and equipment. Light sources are spaced and arranged in a manner that will illuminate the workplace uniformly, without shadows or dark spots.

Color

Colors are used to enhance the worker's feeling of well-being and consequently his work performance. Since the psychological aspects of color were described in Chapter 7, only general comments on the use of colors at workplaces will be made.

The use of warm colors are discouraged for general painting of workplace areas because they tend to tire the eyes after a period of time. Blue and green are much easier on the eyes. Pure colors are also hard on the eyes and should be toned down, especially in areas where a lot of close work is to be done. The use of pure white in any area along the worker's line of sight is discouraged because of its reflectance quality.

Another use of color in work areas is for color-coding. Red can be used to identify moving parts of equipment or other dangerous components. Green is commonly used for first aid equipment. Steps, landings and platforms coded with yellow paint can reduce tripping and falling. Color-coding of various forms helps in identification and minimizes errors.

Noise

Noise levels of 50 decibels or less are recommended for work areas. Somewhat higher levels may be tolerated for a short period of time but continued exposure to high noise levels leads to short-tempered, quarrelsome and dissatisfied workers. Most sources of noise can be prevented or controlled at acceptable levels by proper design. Sources of noise are classified as follows:

(1) Impact noises resulting from contact between hard objects, such as metal utensils banged against metal sinks, or pieces of china banged against each other.

(2) Gear noises caused by the contact of moving parts of equipment and machinery.

(3) Fluid-flow noises of air, water or gases produced by fans, pumps and compressors.

(4) Combustion noises resulting from the burning of fuels as in gas cooking equipment or heating equipment.

(5) Magnetic noises produced by transformers and electric motors used for food service equipment.

Effective noise control is achieved by reducing the transmission of air-borne and structurally transmitted noises. Air-borne transmission of noise can be controlled by placing silencing enclosures around the noise source or by using sound-absorbing surfaces to reduce the amount of reverberation. Silencing enclosures must be constructed in such a way that the enclosed piece of equipment or machinery can be operated and maintained. Unfortunately, silencing enclosures cannot always be built for all the noise-producing sources in work areas.

Structurally transmitted noises can be minimized by installing equipment on vibration-isolating mounts. Using plastic dishracks and other containers will reduce both the creation and transmission of noise.

Ventilation

Adequate ventilation of work areas is necessary to remove smoke, odors, moisture and grease-laden vapor and to bring in fresh air. A well-planned ventilating system can reduce the amount of general cleaning and maintenance.

A general recommendation for ventilation of food service work areas is to supply 5 cubic feet per minute of fresh air per square foot of floor space. This recommendation assumes the presence of heat- and moisture-producing equipment in the area. Air vents for the ventilating system are sized and placed to obtain maximum effectiveness without causing drafts. Fresh air should be tempered by air make-up systems based on outside air characteristics. Make-up air can sometimes be drawn from dining areas if a suitable design can be worked out.

Air-conditioning

In warmer climates, air-conditioning of work areas is needed to maintain the desired environmental conditions. The design of air-conditioning systems for food facilities is very complex because of the special requirements of the cooking process. On one hand, heat-producing equipment is used for cooking which introduces unwanted heat into the general work areas. The air-conditioning system, on the other hand, is used to cool the same general work areas. In a sense, the work areas are being heated and cooled at the same time. The air-conditioning system has to be designed with sensitive controls to

TABLE 8.2

CONCEPTS OF MOTION ECONOMY PERTAINING TO THE
DESIGN OF WORKPLACES

---

(1) Materials, tools and equipment are best located within the normal working area of the worker.
(2) Tools and frequently used materials should have a fixed location at the workplace.
(3) Work requiring the use of the eyes should be done within the normal field of vision.
(4) Prepositioning of tools and materials to facilitate the picking-up actions of hands is desirable.
(5) Gravity-feed bins or chutes should be used to deliver incoming materials to the workplace.
(6) Gravity can also be used to deliver outgoing materials.
(7) The height of the work surface that allows either a standing or sitting position is preferable.
(8) The physical environment of the workplace should be conducive to productive motions.
(9) Tools and equipment controls should be designed for easy grasp.
(10) Jigs, fixtures or foot-operated devices should be used to relieve the work of the hands.
(11) Two or more tools should be combined where possible with due regard for the quality of work.
(12) Tools and materials should be so located as to promote good motion patterns of body members.
(13) Equipment should be designed so the inherent capabilities of the body members are fully utilized.

---

maintain the desired environmental conditions without causing an overload for cooking equipment. The rapid cooling of cooked foods exposed to air-conditioned spaces must be taken into account in the design of the system.

CONCEPTS OF MOTION ECONOMY

Although some of the concepts of motion economy have been implied in the discussion of many subjects in this chapter, a separate identification of them will show their application to the design of workplaces. Planners should frequently check their design against these well-known concepts and make changes as needed. The important concepts of motion economy as they pertain to the design of the workplace are given in Table 8.2.

MATERIALS HANDLING

Another field of knowledge that is useful in the design of workplaces deals with the principles of materials handling. Good design requires a system of materials handling that is desirable for each individual workplace, which in turn makes up the materials-handling system for the entire food service facility. Systems for the handling

TABLE 8.3

PRINCIPLES OF MATERIALS HANDLING

(1) Minimize all material movements and storages.
(2) Use the shortest and straightest routes for the movement of materials across the workplace.
(3) Store materials as close to the point of first use as possible.
(4) Minimize handling of materials by workers unless absolutely necessary.
(5) Preposition all materials at the workplace as much as possible to reduce handling effort.
(6) Handle materials in bulk if at all possible.
(7) Provisions should be made to remove scrap, trash and other wastes at the point of creation.
(8) Take advantage of gravity to move materials when feasible.
(9) Use mechanical aids to lift heavy materials that are frequently used at workplaces.
(10) Built-in leveling devices can be used to keep materials at a convenient working height.
(11) Use mechanized conveyors to move materials that follow a fixed route across the workplace if they do not interfere with the work.
(12) Use well-designed containers and tote pans that are easy to pick up and move.
(13) Consider the use of interlocking containers for moving greater loads with ease and safety.
(14) Consider changing the design of the products involved to improve their materials-handling characteristics.

of food, utensils, garbage, dishes, tools, etc., at the workplace can be guided by the principles identified in Table 8.3.

The principles of materials handling should be used to develop the system for moving materials from workplace to workplace as well. The total design of the system for the entire facility has to be unified in order to achieve maximum efficiency of movement.

SUMMARY

The design of the individual workplaces for the food service facility is one of the keys to good overall design. As each workplace is developed, the planner must continually relate his ideas to the operation of the entire facility. The design of a particular workplace is dictated by the movement of workers and materials to and from other workplaces that are adjacent or near it. Even though only one workplace at a time is planned, it is a part of the total design concept that has to be developed.

BIBLIOGRAPHY

AVERY, A. 1965. Human engineering; the institutional kitchen. Cornell Hotel Restaurant Admin. Quart. *6*, No. 1, 74–83.

BLAKER, G. 1965. Facilitating motion economy through well designed equipment. Hospitals *39*, No. 6, 104–107, 110.

KAZARIAN, E. A. 1969. Work Analysis and Design for Hotels, Restaurants and Institutions. Avi Publishing Co., Westport, Conn.

KOTSCHEVAR, L. H. 1968. Some basic factors in food service planning. Cornell Hotel Restaurant Admin. Quart. *9*, No. 1, 104–113.

NADLER, G. 1963. Work Design. Richard D. Irwin, Homewood, Ill.

WOODSON, W. E. 1964. Human Engineering Guide for Equipment Designers. Univ. Calif. Press, Berkeley, Calif.

CHAPTER 9

Equipment Requirements

METHODS

Determining the specific equipment requirements for the proposed food service facility is one aspect of design on which considerable time can be spent. During this part of the planning process, the food service consultant has to estimate accurately the capacity of each of the various types of food service equipment to be used. If these capacity estimates are too low, the result will be delays and bottlenecks in the production process. Estimates that are too high will result in an expensive and inefficient piece of equipment. The food service consultant must be careful to take into account any projected increases in business volume that would require increased equipment capacity, and plan accordingly. Additional decisions regarding the equipment that may be made at this time include the manufacturer, the model number or designation, attachments and other special accessories needed to process the food items.

A systematic method of determining equipment capacity required is to analyze each food item appearing on the menu. If daily-change menus are used, a sampling of typical menus may be sufficient. The first bit of information needed is an estimate of the number of portions that have to be prepared for a particular meal period. This estimate is made for every menu item requiring equipment, including appetizers, entrees, desserts, breads, salads and beverages. Next, the portion size of each of the menu items is identified. (Typical portion sizes are given in Appendix A). Multiplying the estimated number of portions by the portion size will give the total volume of food to be prepared.

The method of preparation and production for each item is then evaluated. Possible alternatives may include items individually prepared to order; items prepared in small batches in anticipation of orders; items prepared in large batches; and items that are partially batch-prepared and finished when orders are received. The batch size is next determined for those items that are to be prepared in batches. The selection of batch size is one way that the food service consultant can control the capacity of the equipment. Smaller and more frequently prepared batches are desirable because they require less equipment capacity and the foods are fresher when served. Some items that can be held well after cooking can be made in larger batches.

For those items to be prepared and cooked to order, the maximum number of portions to be made at one time is estimated on the basis of the number of customers, their menu preferences, and their arrival patterns. Some projects may require estimates of portions to be prepared per time unit. For example, the number of hamburgers per hour would be estimated for high-volume operations that utilize continuous processing instead of batch processing.

The capacity of some types of equipment is designated by the number of pans they can hold. In those cases, the designer will have to convert the total number of portions into number of certain-size pans. Ovens may be selected by the number of 18 by 26 in. bake pans they can hold. There are other methods of designating capacity for certain types of equipment, and the food service consultant has to convert his portion calculations accordingly.

After determining portions, equipment catalogs may be consulted to match the capacity needed for production with the available sizes of standard equipment. The designer is also careful when sizing some equipment that may have a usable capacity that is somewhat less than the stated capacity. Appropriate adjustments are made in the computations to allow for this discrepancy.

Other data required include the total processing time needed for each menu item for a particular piece of equipment and the time of day that the processing can be done. This information is useful in anticipation of possibly scheduling those items that require the same type of equipment through one piece of equipment instead of two or more. Duplication of equipment is avoided unless there is a need for it, such as having separate deep fryers for fish and chicken, or having one slicer in the preparation area and one in the cooking area if the volume of work to be done in each area warrants it.

A complete discussion of selecting and sizing all the different types of food service equipment is beyond the scope of this book. A brief discussion of frequently specified major items of equipment will serve to illustrate this part of the planning process.

BROILERS

Broilers are classified as equipment which utilizes intense radiant heat for rapid cooking of foods. The two common types are the overhead broiler and the under-fired broiler. Other types of specialty broilers and combinations are available. Broilers are available in either gas or electric models.

Overhead Broilers

Heavy-duty overhead broilers have a large grid area and are equipped with large burners for fast broiling. They may be used individually or incorporated into a heavy-duty range section. Three common methods of incorporating the broiler into the range section are:

(1) Having the broiler at the same height as the range tops.

(2) Having the broiler as an integral unit with an overhead oven that is heated by the burners in the broiling compartment.

(3) Having the broiler mounted on a conventional range type oven with or without an overhead oven.

A small broiler referred to as a salamander can be mounted above the top of a heavy-duty range or above a spreader plate as part of a back-shelf assembly. The broiling capacity of the salamander is not as great as that of the regular overhead broiler. It is primarily used for small operations with light broiling loads or as an auxiliary broiler during off-peak hours in larger operations when the main broiler is not in use.

Modern overhead broilers, as shown in Fig. 9.1, usually will heat

FIG. 9.1. HIGH CAPACITY BROILERS ARE USED FOR RAPID MEAT COOKERY

to broiling temperatures in a short time and have pull-out grids for easy loading and unloading. Adequate venting of broilers is required to remove smoke and odors.

Underfired Char Broilers

Char broilers use pieces of ceramic or other refractory materials to form a radiant bed above the burners. The food items are placed on a grate located directly above the radiant bed. While cooking, the juices from foods drip directly on the hot bed and burn, which gives the typical charcoal flavor and appearance. Since a great deal of smoke is given off by char broilers, they must be used under an efficient exhaust hood.

Char broilers are available in multiple sections which increase the grid area for high-capacity broiling.

Approximate cooking times for typical items processed on broilers are given in Table 9.1. These times are used for estimating the grid area of the broiler that is required for the food facility. Cooking

TABLE 9.1

APPROXIMATE COOKING TIMES FOR BROILING

Item	Thickness In.	Approximate Cooking Time (Min)		
		Rare	Medium	Well-Done
Beef				
Steaks	1	15	20	30
	1½	25	35	
	2	35	50	
Ground Beef	1	15	20	
Lamb				
Chops and Steaks	1		12	15
	1½		15	20
	2		20	25
Ground Lamb	1		20	22
Poultry				
Chicken parts				20
Half chickens				30
Pork				
Ham, uncooked	½			15
	1			20
Ham, cooked	½			6
	1			10
Seafood				
Fish, fillets	½			8
	1			12
Fish, whole	2			20
	3			25
Lobster tails				12

times vary with many factors, including initial temperature of the food and closeness to the heat source. Consequently these times should be used only for estimating equipment capacity.

To determine the broiler capacity required for a particular menu item, the designer will estimate the total number of portions that would have to be placed on the broiler grid at one time. Knowing the approximate area per portion, the total area required can be computed. If more than one type of food item is to be processed, then each type is checked to see which item will generate the greatest demand on the broiler. If the production estimates are in terms of portions per hour, the average cooking time is considered and the capacity of the broiler is based on this factor.

DEEP FRYERS

Deep-fat fryers are generally divided into three categories. One category includes conventional open-type fryers which range from a small 11 by 11-in. fat kettle to a 24 by 24-in. fat kettle. The capacity of fryers is indicated in pounds of fat. This designation implies the amount of fat to be used in the fryer. Fat capacity designations for conventional fryers vary from 15 to 130 lb. Conventional fryers, as shown in Fig. 9.2, may be free-standing or can be built-in. Counter models are available for small requirements.

Pressure fryers make up another category of deep fryers. Pressure fryers are equipped with lids that can be sealed to permit pressure to build up within the kettle. This type of fryer is ideal for certain specialty items such as deep-fried chicken.

The last category of deep fryers is the continuous-type fryer. These fryers are equipped with a screw conveyor that continuously moves the product through the fat. Items that require a longer frying time are placed at the extreme end of the conveyor so they traverse a greater distance, and hence have a longer time in the fat.

Fryer capacity is sometimes estimated by assuming that a fryer can process from 1.5 to 2 times its weight of fat per hour. For example, a 50-lb fryer should be able to fry from 75 to 100 lb of food per hour. An alternative method of determining fryer capacity is to determine the actual weight of the food item to be fried per hour and compare this figure with capacity specifications provided by the manufacturer. Most manufacturers will supply capacity information for a variety of food items, such as potatoes, chicken and shrimp.

Typical frying times for conventional deep fryers are shown in Table 9.2. These times may be used to estimate the number of batches per hour that can be produced. Times for loading, draining

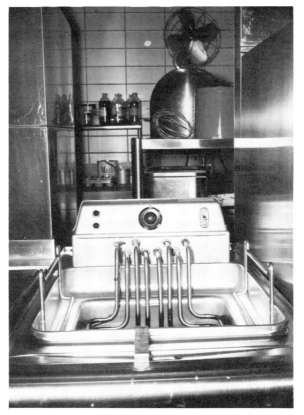

FIG. 9.2. A CONVENTIONAL FRYER FOR DEEP FRY-
ING FOODS

and unloading are estimated and added to the cooking times to obtain the total batch time.

Since the frying time for many items is quite short, an automatic
basket-lift or at least a timer bell is desirable. This allows cooks to
attend other needs without consistently having to check the fryer.

GRIDDLES

Griddles are flat-top pieces of equipment heated from beneath, as
compared to grills which have heating sources both above and beneath. Griddles are used for high-production food service and fast-
food operations. Grills are more of a specialty piece of equipment.

Griddles are available in a variety of sizes from as small as 7 in.
wide and 14 in. deep to as large as 72 in. wide and 24 in. deep. Both
gas-fired and electric models are suitable for most purposes. Typical

TABLE 9.2

APPROXIMATE FRYING TIMES FOR
CONVENTIONAL FRYERS

Food Item	Frying Time (Min)
Chicken	
Raw pieces	10–15
Fritters	3–4
Sea foods	
Fish fillets	3–5
Clams	3–4
Scallops	3–5
Shrimp	3–4
Oysters	3–5
Vegetables	
Potatoes, $\frac{1}{4}$ in. cut	4–6
Potatoes, $\frac{3}{8}$ in. cut	5–7
Potatoes, $\frac{1}{2}$ in. cut	6–8
Cauliflower	2–4
Eggplant	5–7
Onions	2–3
Miscellaneous	
Doughnuts	2–3
Corn on the cob	3–4
Meat turnovers	5–7
French toast	2–3

foods and the approximate cooking times on griddles are given in Table 9.3.

Griddle capacity is designated by the physical dimensions of the cooking surface. Griddle capacity required is determined by the same

TABLE 9.3

APPROXIMATE COOKING TIMES
FOR GRIDDLING

Food Item	Cooking Time (Min)
Bacon	5–6
Beef tenderloin	6–8
Bologna	2–3
Grilled cheese	1–2
Eggs	2–3
Fried potatoes	3–4
Hamburgers	2–5
Ham loaf	2–3
Ham steak	8–10
Minute steak	3–5
Pancakes	2–3
Sausage	3–5

method suggested for broilers. Manufacturers will frequently have production capacity stated in terms of certain food items.

Griddles can be free-standing, counter-mounted, mobile or built-in as the situation demands. Thermostatic controls which maintain constant surface temperatures are necessary for proper operation of the griddle. The height of splash guards and the location and width of grease troughs should be considered when specifying griddles.

OVENS

Ovens are available in a great variety of types, sizes and methods of operation. Different types may be used to bake, roast, oven-broil, oven-fry, cook casseroles and reconstitute frozen foods. The capacities of ovens are stated in terms of the cooking chamber dimensions or by the number of bake or roast pans that can be placed in the oven at one time. Some operations may require more than one oven to handle the different temperature and time requirements of their menu items.

Deck Ovens

Deck ovens, as the name implies, can be decked or stacked to increase capacity without using additional floor space. Deck ovens may be either roasting or baking ovens. Roasting ovens have chambers that are 12 to 15 in. high while baking decks are usually 8 in. high. Both types of ovens are available in a wide range of chamber lengths and widths. The approximate roasting times for meat items are given in Table 9.4. Cooking times are used to estimate the oven capacity required by computing the number of batches per hour that can be handled. Baking times for typical baked goods are shown in Table 9.5.

TABLE 9.4

APPROXIMATE ROASTING TIMES FOR MEATS

Meat	Approximate Cooking Time Per Lb (Min)
Beef	
Rare	20–30
Medium	24–40
Well-done	28–50
Veal	25–35
Lamb	30–35
Pork, fresh	30–50
Ham, uncooked	20–25
Ham, cooked	15–18

TABLE 9.5

APPROXIMATE BAKING TIMES

Food Item	Baking Time (Min)
Bread	30–35
Cakes	20–25
Cookies	15–20
Pastry	
Pie shells	20–25
Puff pastry	25–30
Eclairs	25–30
Turnovers	25–30
Pies	
Fruit	50–60
Meringue	15–20
Pumpkin	30–35
Custard	30–35
Rolls	15–20
Buns	20–25

Baking and roasting decks may be combined in any desired arrangement. For best performance, each deck can be equipped with its own burner and thermostat. Less expensive arrangements using one burner and thermostat for two or more decks are available.

The two-deck oven is preferred for ease of use and safety. The top deck of a three-deck arrangement is usually too high for safe and easy reach, while the bottom deck requires considerable bending to load and unload.

Convection Ovens

Convection ovens differ from other ovens in that a fan is used to provide rapid circulation of heated air within the chamber. This permits foods to be cooked on multiple racks instead of on a hearth; consequently almost the entire volume of oven space can be utilized. This results in an increased production capacity. Rapid air circulation also maintains an even temperature in all parts of the oven chamber.

Since heat transfer into the food products is increased by the forced convection, a lower temperature and shorter cooking time may be used. Lower temperatures will minimize the shrinkage of roasts.

Revolving-tray Ovens

Revolving-tray ovens use flat trays suspended between two reels that rotate the trays. Food items to be roasted or baked are loaded on the trays as they appear opposite the door opening. The ovens are designed to prevent the escape of hot air when the door is opened for loading or unloading. One advantage of the revolving-tray oven is that its high capacity allows several menu items to be cooked simultaneously.

Most ovens are built with 4 to 7 trays, the tray sizes varying from as little as 18 by 30 in. to as much as 26 by 108 in. The larger capacities are best suited to institutional or commissary type operations. Capacity is designated by the total number of pans that can be loaded into the oven at one time.

Microwave Ovens

Microwave ovens cook foods by converting microwave energy into heat energy within the food. The energy is created by electronic microwave tubes placed in the cooking chamber. As the microwave energy is emitted it is absorbed by the foods and converted into heat. Characteristics of various foods dictate how long it will take to fully cook them. Cooking time is reduced considerably in comparison to other types of ovens. The quick heating capacity of microwave ovens makes them ideal for reconstituting frozen foods.

As with other ovens, capacity is dependent upon the volume of the cooking chamber and the cooking time required. With the shorter cooking time, microwave ovens have a higher output per hour than other similar-sized ovens. Microwave ovens are available in a number of compartment sizes and in a continuous type. Typical processing times for a variety of food items are given in Table 9.6.

Infrared Ovens

Infrared ovens operate on a principle somewhat similar to microwave ovens. The basic difference is that the infrared oven uses infrared energy waves, which have shorter wavelengths than microwaves. In an infrared oven, the energy waves are directed to the food, where they are absorbed and converted into heat. The penetration of infrared energy into the food is not very deep and consequently the cooking process is similar to conventional ovens. Microwaves penetrate much deeper into the food than infrared waves. An advantage of both infrared and microwave ovens is that the air enclosed in the oven chamber is not heated by the radiant energy. This characteristic of introducing energy into the food directly without heating the air makes it a highly efficient method of heat transfer.

The characteristics of the infrared oven make it suitable for both regular cooking of raw foods and for reheating or reconstituting frozen items. The time required for cooking raw items in an infrared

TABLE 9.6

APPROXIMATE PROCESSING TIMES FOR MICROWAVE OVENS

Food Item	Processing Time (Min)
Meat, precooked and cooled	
Ham steak	3
Short ribs of beef	2
Poultry, precooked and cooled	
Fried chicken, disjointed	$2\frac{1}{2}$
Fried chicken, half	$2\frac{1}{2}$
Seafood, raw to done	2
Vegetables, canned	
Corn, green beans, peas	$\frac{1}{2}$
Baked beans	$\frac{3}{4}$
Potatoes	$1\frac{1}{4}$
Vegetables, fresh	
Corn on the cob	2
Broccoli	8
Spinach	3
Asparagus	9
Potatoes	5
Vegetables, frozen	
Corn	5
Asparagus	7
Cauliflower	12
Casseroles, precooked and cooled	
Chicken a la king	$1\frac{1}{2}$
Stuffed cabbage	2
Macaroni and cheese	$1\frac{3}{4}$
Spanish rice	$1\frac{1}{2}$
Spaghetti.	$1\frac{1}{2}$
Beef Stew	2
Ravioli	2
Chili con carne	$1\frac{3}{4}$
Meat pie	$1\frac{3}{4}$
Chop suey	2

oven is less than in conventional ovens. Reconstitution of frozen foods in infrared ovens takes somewhat longer than in microwave ovens.

Infrared ovens are a fairly new development and the sizes available are limited to smaller units. For this reason, infrared ovens are frequently used as auxiliary or back-up units to other types of equipment.

PREPARATION EQUIPMENT

Food Cutters

Food cutters are versatile pieces of equipment that can handle meats, vegetables and fruits. The food cutter can cut, dice, shred and almost liquefy foods, depending upon the amount of time the food is left in the cutter. The foods to be size-reduced are placed in a bowl which rotates and exposes them to high-speed rotating blades. The capacity of cutters is measured by the size of the bowl or by the amount of food that can be processed per minute. Both bench and floor models are available. Some cutter models are equipped with an attachment hub for accepting various attachments.

Slicers

The basic design of food slicers includes a circular knife blade and a carriage that passes under the blade. Foods to be sliced are placed on the carriage and are either hand-fed or automatically fed. A very close adjustment and consequent control of thickness of the slices can be obtained with slicers.

Mixers

The primary function of a mixer is to mix; however, it can perform a variety of other functions by using accessories and attachments. Mixer capacity is indicated by the capacity of the bowl. Bench models are sized from 5 to 20 qt; larger floor models range from 30 to 400-qt capacity. Most mixers have adapter rings enabling them to handle different-sized bowls. Larger models can be obtained with bowl-raising and lowering mechanisms to simplify handling large bowls.

Mixers are designed to operate at a variety of rotational speeds, depending on the job. Accessories available include various whips, beaters and knives attached directly to the drive shaft. Attachments, which permit the mixer to perform other functions, are adaptable only to the mixers that have an attachment hub. Available attachments include a food chopper, dicer, slicer, juice extractor, tool sharpener and a variety of shredder and grater plates.

Vertical Cutter/Mixer

The vertical cutter/mixer is basically a stationary bowl with horizontal blades that rotate at high speed. The capacity of a vertical cutter/mixer is much greater than the typical food cutter and is suitable for large-volume operations. Capacity is designated by the bowl size and ranges from 25 to 60 qt.

Vegetable Peelers

Vegetable peelers are cylindrical tanks that have a revolving disc at the bottom. The tank is equipped with two openings, one above the disc for loading vegetables and one below it for removing the peels.

Depending upon the model, the disc or the walls, or in some cases both, are coated with an abrasive. As the disc revolves, the vegetables are thrown against the abrasive, which peels the skin. Water is introduced to keep the abrasive surface clean and to carry away the peeled skins to the lower opening. Peeling time varies with the type of vegetable and may be from 30 seconds to 4 minutes.

Capacity of peelers is designated by the quantity of vegetables that can be placed in the peeler. Capacities from 15 to 70 lb are typical. Some manufacturers designate capacity by relating it to the horsepower rating of the electric motor.

RANGES

The advent of new processed foods and new equipment, coupled with the shortage of skilled chefs, have relieved the need for a large battery of ranges for many types of food service facilities. The range is still a favorite for operations that feature cook-to-order items and home-made menu items.

Heavy-duty ranges are designed to meet the requirements of continuous high production volumes. Restaurant-type ranges are of lighter construction and do not have the durability for continuing heavy production requirements; they are suggested for smaller operations or for limited-use applications.

A variety of range designs are available, including solid tops, open tops and griddle tops. Most ranges will have ovens under, although models with shelves or storage cabinets under are used in some cases.

Range sections are usually 29 to 37 in. wide and from 34 to 42 in. deep. Sections are joined to give any desirable range top area to meet the requirements of the food facility.

STEAM-JACKETED KETTLES

Steam-jacketed kettles are constructed of two bowls sealed one within the other, with about 2 in. of space between them for the introduction of steam. The amount of steam surface between the bowls is referred to as jacketing, and models from half-jacketed to full-jacketed types are available. The operation of steam-jacketed kettles utilizes steam which is condensed back to water in the jacket to provide the heat for the inner kettle. A condensate line is provided to remove the water that accumulates. The amount of heat input is dependent upon the pressure and amount of steam allowed to enter the jacketed area.

Smaller steam-jacketed kettles may be mounted on tables or counters; larger models are mounted to the floor or wall. Many models can be tilted for easy removal of contents. Capacity designations are in quarts for smaller models and gallons for larger models. The usable capacity of steam-jacketed kettles is generally figured to be 75% of stated capacity.

STEAMERS

Steamers are basically sealed compartments where steam is allowed to come in direct contact with the food for cooking. Conventional steamers operate with steam at a pressure of 5 psi, which corresponds to a temperature of 227° F. These steamers are referred to as large-compartment steamers and are capable of producing large volumes of food.

High-pressure steamers, sometimes called speed-cookers, are smaller units that operate with steam at a pressure of 15 psi. The resultant temperature in the high-pressure steamer is approximately 250° F. A single-unit high-pressure steamer is illustrated in Fig. 9.3.

FIG. 9.3. HIGH PRESSURE STEAMERS ARE IDEAL FOR QUICK PREPARATION OF VEGETABLES AND OTHER FOODS

TABLE 9.7

APPROXIMATE PROCESSING TIMES FOR STEAMERS

Food Items	Approximate Processing Time (Min)	
	Conventional Steamer	High-Pressure Steamer
Vegetables, fresh		
Asparagus	6–8	1–1½
Beans, green	20–25	2–3
Beans, lima	10–12	1–2
Broccoli	7–10	1–3
Carrots, sliced	12–15	2–5
Cauliflower, pieces	8–10	2–3
Corn, kernel	6–8	2–3
Peas	4–5	1–1½
Potatoes, quartered	18–24	5–10
Tomatoes	4–5	½–2
Vegetables, frozen		
Asparagus	4–6	2–3
Beans, green	15–18	2–3
Beans, lima	8–10	1–2½
Broccoli	4–6	1–2
Carrots, sliced	10–12	2–3
Cauliflower	6–8	1½–2½
Peas	3–4	1–1½
Seafood, frozen		
Shrimp		10–12
Lobster tails		7–8
Poultry, fresh		
Chicken, pieces		4–5

The capacity of a steamer is designated by the number of steamer pans that can be placed in it at one time. Usual capacities range from units that can hold three 12 by 20-in. pans to those having a capacity of 18 pans. An unusual designation of bushels is sometimes used to indicate steamer capacity; this implies the bushels of vegetables that can be cooked at one time in the steamer.

Typical processing times for some foods for conventional and high-pressure steamers are given in Table 9.7. These times may be used to determine the number of batches that can be processed per hour.

Steamers are ideal for vegetable cookery because they retain the color and textures without undue shrinkage. Both fresh and frozen vegetables may be steamed.

WAREWASHING EQUIPMENT

Dishwashers are the major item of equipment for warewashing and are generally classified by the number of tanks. A single-tank dishwasher is the smallest-capacity machine and is used for limited facilities. Counter-service operations frequently use single-tank dishwashers that are either bench-mounted or placed under counters or work tables. Most single-tank dishwashers have only a wash-and-rinse cycle.

Two-tank dishwashers are used for greater loads, and are available in rack or rackless models. They usually have a power wash cycle, power rinse cycle and a final rinse cycle. Some models may omit the power rinse and have a pre-wash cycle instead. The discharge sections are designed to allow sufficient drying of dinnerware before it is handled.

Larger three-tank dishwashers have power pre-wash, wash and rinse sections and many are designed for a final rinse cycle as well.

Dishwasher capacity is stated in terms of numbers of pieces of dinnerware that can be washed per hour. Some manufacturers also have recommendations of size based on the number of meals to be served per meal period. For example, a single-tank dishwasher will be suitable for washing dinnerware from 50 to 600 meals per meal period. Two-tank machines are capable of handling dinnerware from 1500 to 2000 meals per meal period. Three-tank dishwashers are usually rated for 2500 meals. These recommendations are guides, and the actual capacity required for a particular operation will depend on the number of each type of dinnerware to be washed and the time allowed for washing.

Some operations may prefer separate glasswashers, especially if large numbers are to be washed daily. Small glasswashers are frequently located in bar areas and in counter units.

WASTE DISPOSALS

Most waste disposal units operate by using water to carry the wastes into shredders that cut it into small pieces. As the size of the pieces is reduced to about one-eighth inch, they are flushed into the sewer. Some large disposals have a screw-type shaft that forces the waste into the shredders. Waste disposals are sized according to the horsepower of the motor. Typical sizes available range from 0.33 to 5.0 horsepower.

Waste disposal units are frequently installed at points where garbage and wastes are generated. Locations such as soiled dish tables, pot and pan washing areas and preparation areas are usual waste-disposal installation points. Optional accessories for the disposal units include silver trappers and overhead spray units for washing waste directly into the disposal.

EQUIPMENT SELECTION

Selecting a particular make and model of any type of equipment is the final step in determining equipment requirements. Food service consultants will prepare a "schedule of equipment" which will list the specific equipment to be used for the facility. The following points are considered in deciding the make and model of equipment to specify:

(1) simplicity of operation;
(2) sanitary design;
(3) modular sizes to fit standard-sized pans;
(4) ease of installation;
(5) cost of operation;
(6) ease of repair and maintenance;
(7) durability;
(8) compatibility with other equipment.

The design of the equipment should be simple, functional and attractive. Maximum utility at a reasonable cost is to be sought for all types of equipment.

BIBLIOGRAPHY

ANOFF, I. S. 1972. Food Service Equipment Industry. Institutions/Volume Feeding Magazine, Chicago.
ANON. 1965. The menu; your guide to equipment buying. Volume Feeding Management 24, No. 3, 25–50.
KOTSCHEVAR, L. H. 1964. Quantity Food Production. Edwards Brothers, Ann Arbor, Mich.
KOTSCHEVAR. L. H., and TERRELL, M. E. 1961. Food Service Planning. John Wiley & Sons, New York.
SCHMID, F. 1963. Kitchen layout and equipment selection. Cooking For Profit 32, No. 10, 52–56, 86.
STOKES, J. W. 1967. How to Manage a Restaurant. Wm. C. Brown Co., Dubuque, Iowa.
WILKINSON, J. 1964. The Complete Book of Cooking Equipment. Institutions Magazine, Chicago.

CHAPTER 10

Space Requirements

INTRODUCTION

Accurate determination of the space requirements for a food service facility is a very difficult problem, involving considerable research and computation. The space required for each functional area of the facility is dependent upon many factors which are not constant for all types of operations. The factors involved include the number of meals to be prepared; the functions and tasks to be performed; the equipment requirements; the number of employees and corresponding workplaces required; storage for materials; and suitable space for traffic and movement. The importance of accurately evaluating these factors cannot be overemphasized. Overestimating or underestimating any of them can lead to an excess or a shortage of space for the facility.

SPACE ESTIMATES

The general guides and "rules of thumb" that will be given are to be used for preliminary space estimates only. They are to be regarded as strictly tentative and subject to easy change. The "rules of thumb" are used to get a general idea of the overall size of a facility in order to make preliminary cost estimates for feasibility studies, or to determine approximate land requirements for the building. One problem with using guides and "rules of thumb" is that the figures given are usually based on existing operations and do not reflect newer methods of food service operation. Another difficulty is that these figures are not given for all types of food service operations and consequently they would be of little use for certain types of projects. Most of the figures available are for general facilities that have no unusual space requirements.

TOTAL FACILITY SIZE

Depending upon the type of food service facility to be planned, a general estimate of the total building size can be obtained by relating it to the number of seats to be provided. The estimated square footage of total space per seat is given in Table 10.1. These figures can be related to the number of meals to be prepared by considering the turnover rate for a particular meal period. A range of space estimates is given to allow for variations in the methods of operation. The

TABLE 10.1

ESTIMATED TOTAL FACILITY SPACE
FOR FOOD SERVICE FACILITIES

Type of Operation	Area Per Seat (Sq Ft)
Table service	24–32
Counter service	18–24
Booth service	20–28
Cafeteria service	22–30

smaller figures are used for limited menu and limited-space operations; the larger figures are suitable for operations with extensive menus and allow more spacious areas.

Figures for estimating the total facility size of other types of food service, such as tray service, car service or take-out service, are not available because of the great variations that exist in these types of operations. The only guides available would be to evaluate similar existing operations and make adjustments as needed.

DINING AREAS

Estimating the space required for dining areas is based on the number of persons to be seated at one time and the square feet of space allowed per seat. The number of persons to be seated at one time is determined by considering the total number of customers to be served for a given time period, and the turnover. Turnover refers to seat usage and is expressed by the number of times a seat will be occupied over a given time period. Turnover is usually expressed on a per-hour basis, although it can be determined on a per meal basis. The turnover is determined by estimating the average time a seat is occupied for the time period desired. For example, if the turnover is to be expressed on a per-hour basis and the average estimated time the seat is occupied is 20 minutes, the turnover is 3. If the average seat occupancy time is 30 min, then the turnover rate is 2 per hour. Determining the turnover rate per meal period is useful for determining the total seating capacity based on estimated sales volume.

Turnover rates are affected by the method of serving and serving time as well as by the type of customer, menu offerings and the dining atmosphere. Typical turnover rates for some types of food service operations are shown in Table 10.2.

Turnover rates can be increased to some extent by many design and operational factors. This is not to suggest that all facilities should be designed for high turnover rates. However, if high turnover is one of

TABLE 10.2

TURNOVER RATES FOR FOOD SERVICE FACILITIES

Type of Operation	Turnover Rate (Per Hr)
Commercial cafeteria	$1\frac{1}{2}-2\frac{1}{2}$
Industrial or school cafeterias	2–3
Counter service	$2-3\frac{1}{2}$
Combination counter and table service	2–3
Leisurely table service	$\frac{1}{2}-1$
Regular table service	$1-2\frac{1}{2}$

the basic objectives, then the planner and subsequent manager can use the following to accomplish this:

(1) Use menu items that require short processing times, or use predominately preprocessed items.
(2) Provide ample production space and equipment to handle the peak periods.
(3) Use well-lighted and light-colored painted areas for serving and dining.
(4) Arrange dining tables in close proximity to each other.
(5) Develop a somewhat uncomfortable dining seat design.
(6) Provide sufficient service personnel so guests are served promptly after they are seated.
(7) Provide for prompt clearing of the tables when a customer is finished with a course or the entire meal.
(8) Make sure guest checks are presented to customers as soon as they are finished eating.

FIG. 10.1. DINING ROOMS SHOULD BE SIZED TO PRO-VIDE SUFFICIENT ROOM FOR TABLES AND CHAIRS WITHOUT CROWDING

Note that a number of factors identified above are characteristic of the management policy after the facility has been built. This again emphasizes the close working relationship that has to exist between the owner or manager and the planner during the planning process. A food service facility designed for high turnover must also be managed for high turnover if the anticipated volume of sales is to be generated.

The square feet of space allowed in the dining areas is governed by the amount of comfort desired. Crowding in dining areas is not desirable except in some quick-service fast-food operations. Most individuals would like to have sufficient elbow room and table space to enjoy their meal. The dining area shown in Fig. 10.1 provides ample space for the customers. Suggested space requirements for dining areas are given in Table 10.3. The figures on the high end of the

TABLE 10.3

ESTIMATED DINING AREA SPACE
FOR FOOD SERVICE FACILITIES

Type of Facility	Dining Space Per Seat (Sq Ft)
Table service	12–18
Counter service	16–20
Booth service	12–16
Cafeteria service	12–16
Banquet	10–12

range are used where ample space or leisurely dining are to be provided. The figures on the low end of the range will result in minimum space requirements.

The estimates for dining areas include space for tables, chairs, aisles and service stations. They do not allow for waiting areas, rest rooms or other similar areas. Space requirements for these areas have to be determined separately. The size and arrangement of tables, chairs, booths and counters selected for the dining area are important to the efficient use of the space allowed.

PRODUCTION AREAS

The space estimates for production areas include room for all the functional areas, such as receiving, storage, preparation, cooking and warewashing, that are required to produce the menu items. Estimates for production areas for typical food service facilities are given in Table 10.4.

TABLE 10.4

ESTIMATED PRODUCTION SPACE
FOR FOOD FACILITIES

Type of Facility	Space Per Seat (Sq Ft)
Table service	8-12
Counter service	4-6
Booth service	6-10
Cafeteria service	8-12

Facilities that will be processing primarily fresh items should use the higher space estimates. This allows for the additional equipment and worker space needed. The smaller figures are used for operations using preprocessed foods and require minimal production space.

A suggested percentage breakdown of the production space for general table service operations is shown in Table 10.5.

TABLE 10.5

ESTIMATED PERCENTAGE OF PRODUCTION
SPACE ALLOWED FOR
FUNCTIONAL AREAS

Functional Area	Space Allowed (%)
Receiving	5
Food storage	20
Preparation	14
Cooking	8
Baking	10
Warewashing	5
Traffic aisles	16
Trash storage	5
Employee facilities	15
Miscellaneous	2

These percentage figures assume a typical operation using fresh products. Baking of rolls, pastries and cakes are also assumed to be done in the facility.

SPACE CALCULATIONS

Another approach to the problem of determining space requirements is to calculate the space needed for each of the functional areas separately. This is done by identifying and determining the pertinent variables involved for the different functional areas. It is assumed at this point that the individual workplaces and pieces of equipment for the facility have been determined and will now be grouped together. The space required for the flow of materials and workers between the workplaces and pieces of equipment is added as needed to develop the space to allow for each function.

A brief discussion of some of the functional areas and the variables affecting their space requirements will be given to illustrate this procedure. Computational operations are presented as applicable. Consideration of the traffic aisles is one of the common variables for all areas and is therefore included.

Traffic Aisles

Traffic aisles are used for the movement of materials and workers, and should not be confused with work aisles which provide floor space for the worker to perform his task. The primary purpose of traffic aisles is to allow easy movement between workplaces, equipment and functional areas. Since traffic aisles are not productive space, they should be kept at a minimum both in numbers and size. Traffic aisles, as shown in Fig. 10.2, should be just wide enough to provide easy movement of the materials and workers required for efficient operation of the facility.

In general, work aisles and traffic aisles should be separated as much as possible. This can usually be accomplished by locating traffic aisles perpendicular to the work aisles. In some instances, combined work and traffic aisles may be used if the traffic is light and if they offer a better solution to the design problem. Traffic aisles that serve two or more functional areas will minimize the amount of space required. Placement of traffic aisles along walls and other perimeter locations is not desirable for the same reason.

The width of traffic aisles is dependent upon the type of traffic to be accommodated. If it consists of only people who are not carrying anything, a minimum aisle width of 30 in. will allow persons to pass without difficulty. For workers who will be carrying containers and materials or pushing mobile carts and trucks an aisle width of 24 in. plus the width of the container or material carried or the mobile cart width will allow enough space. For example, if one worker has to pass another worker pushing a 20-in. wide cart, an aisle width of 44 in. (24 plus 20) would be needed. The traffic aisle widths required for special types of movement such as carrying large trays have to be sized accordingly.

In those instances where a combined work and traffic aisle is needed, a minimum of 42 in. is required to allow one person to pass another person at his workplace. Aisles where there are persons working in a back-to-back arrangement have to be a minimum of 48

FIG. 10.2. TRAFFIC AISLES ARE SIZED TO HANDLE
THE   FLOW   OF   MATERIALS   AND   WORKERS
EFFICIENTLY

in. wide to allow passage of people betweem them. An important
point to remember is that the less movement required to operate the
facility, the less aisle space is needed.

RECEIVING AREA

The main variables affecting the amount of space needed for the
receiving function are the number, type and size of deliveries that are

to be handled at one time. Many operations can have deliveries scheduled so they will have to handle only one delivery at a time. The types of materials to be received are considered because of the variety of containers and packaging methods available. Ease of opening, checking, moving and stackability all have a bearing on the space required.

The size of deliveries to be handled may depend on the storage space available in the facility, and is determined in conjunction with storage space requirements. Storage space in turn can be modified by the frequency of deliveries. A greater frequency of deliveries can reduce the size requirements of the receiving area as well. Therefore, storage space and receiving space requirements should be determined together after these factors have been evaluated.

Needless to say, all equipment and work areas for the receiving function must be provided for.

STORAGE AREAS

The amount of dry, refrigerator and freezer space required for the facility is determined by the number of days of storage to be provided for. A general recommendation for dry storage of foods is to provide space for 2 to 4 weeks supply, depending on the availability of the food items. The total volume of goods to be stored can be estimated as follows. First determine the number of meals for which storage is to be provided. An operation planning on serving 600 meals per day and desiring a two weeks supply will need storage for 8400 (600 meals per day × 14 days) meals. Next, estimate the weight per meal of items that will be stored in the dry storage area. This calls for an evaluation of all menu items. A general estimate between $1/4$ to $1/2$ lb per meal may be used; it is based on a total weight estimate per average meal of 1 to $1^1/_2$ lb. These figures are for full meals and adjustments for partial meals have to be made. If an estimate of $1/2$ lb per meal is used, then the total weight to provide storage for is 4,200 lb (8400 meals × 0.5 lb per meal). Then the total weight computed is divided by an average density of 45 lb per cubic ft, which will give the total volume of goods to be stored. In this example, the total volume in cubic feet is: 4200 lb ÷ 45 lb/cubic ft = 93.3. This indicates that space for 93.3 cubic ft of goods, exclusive of aisle space, will be needed.

If the goods are to be stored on shelves, the total square footage of shelving can be computed by considering the height to which the materials can be stored on the shelf. If the materials can be stored to a height of 1 ft, then 93.3 (93.3 cubic ft ÷ 1 foot) sq ft of shelving will be needed. If a height of $1^1/_2$ feet can be used, then 62.2 (93.3 ÷ 1.5) sq ft of shelving is required. The length of shelving is computed by dividing the square feet by the width of shelving to be used.

This same method of computation can be used for the refrigerator and freezer storage areas. The weight per meal of items that will be stored in the refrigerators and freezers will vary between 0.75 and 1 lb. The average density of refrigerator items can be assumed to be 30 lb per cubic ft. Items that will be stored in freezers can be assumed to have a density of 40 lb per cubic ft.

The number of days of storage for refrigerator items may vary from one day to a week or more, depending on the method of operation used for the facility. Freezer items can be stored for longer periods of time and are determined by the frequency of deliveries available. An economic lot size analysis may be made to determine the optimum size of storage to provide. The analysis compares ordering, purchasing and receiving costs to the cost of the storage.

SERVING AREAS

Serving areas for most table service facilities are planned as a part of the main cooking area and separate space determinations are not usually needed. The pick-up area shown in Fig. 10.3 is included in the space requirements for the main cooking area. Additional serving stations for table service can be considered in computations for the dining area.

FIG. 10.3. FACILITIES FOR SERVING IN TABLE SERVICE OPERATIONS INCLUDE PICK-UP COUNTERS AT THE MAIN COOKING AREA

Cafeteria operations require separate space for the serving function to allow room for the serving counter, room for guests and room for servers. Variables affecting the size of the serving area are the number of people to be served and the serving time allowed. Serving line rates vary from 2 to 10 persons per minute for straight-line cafeteria counters. The serving line rate is dependent on the number of choices and the number of servers. Shopping-center counter arrangements can handle up to 20 or more persons per minute.

The length of cafeteria counters is determined by the variety and volume of food items to be displayed. Adequate space for merchandising food items, as shown in Fig. 10.4, should be allowed.

FIG. 10.4. LENGTH OF CAFETERIA COUNTERS SHOULD ALLOW SUFFI-
CIENT SPACE TO MERCHANDISE FOODS

The space required for straight-line counters may be roughly estimated at 10 to 15 sq ft of floor space for each linear foot of counter. This provides room for the counters, customer aisles, room for servers and back-bar equipment. Shopping-center arrangements generally require 18 to 20 sq ft of floor area for each linear foot of counter.

The sizing of serving facilities for cafeterias is directly related to the capacity of the dining area. Ideal design results when the flow of people from the serving facility is balanced with the seating available in the dining room. At equilibrium conditions, the flow rate of people leaving the serving areas and entering the dining area should equal the flow rate of people leaving the dining area. In other words, the number of seats provided in the dining area has a direct relationship to the rate of people leaving the serving line for a given average eating time. This relationship can be expressed by the equation:

$$R = \frac{N}{T}$$

where R = rate of people leaving serving area
N = number of seats in dining area
T = average eating time.

For example, a 200-seat dining room where the average eating time is 20 minutes should have serving facilities capable of handling $10 \left(R = \dfrac{200}{20} \right)$ persons per minute. If the eating time is 30 minutes, a serving facility must be able to handle $6.7 \left(R = \dfrac{200}{30} \right)$ persons per minute.

These procedures illustrate the preferred method of arriving at space requirements for a food service facility. Each type of food facility to be planned will have differences that will result in different space requirements.

BIBLIOGRAPHY

ANON. 1967. Allocating space. Institutions *60*, No. 2, 122–123.
KOTSCHEVAR, L. H., and TERRELL, M. E. 1961. Food Service Planning. John Wiley & Sons, New York.
MILLER, E. 1966. Profitable Cafeteria Operation. Ahrens Book Co., New York.
SCHNEIDER, N. F., JOHN, E. A., and SMITH, A. Q. 1962. Commercial Kitchens. American Gas Assoc., New York.

CHAPTER 11

Layout of Facilities

SPACE ARRANGEMENT

After developing the workplaces, determining the specific equipment to use and finalizing the space requirements, the food facility designer is ready to accomplish the layout phase of the planning process. Actually, this has probably been developing in the designer's mind as he was accomplishing the various other planning steps. Some of the equipment layouts for certain functions may already have been completed during the design of the workplaces. Now the designer will formalize them, first as rough sketches, and ultimately in the form of blueprints.

The layout process may be described as two separate stages that occur at the same time. One stage deals with the arrangement of individual pieces of equipment, work tables and sinks into a unit which comprise a functional area or a functional department. The term department is sometimes associated with separate rooms, but this is not necessarily the case with food service operations. In essence, the designer is developing an area where related functions will be performed, and he may include as many or as few functions as deemed appropriate for the project. To illustrate, one particular area may be developed for the functions of dessert preparation, salad preparation and sandwich preparation, whereas another project may require three separate areas for these functions.

The second stage of the layout process involves arranging the functional areas or departments into the total facility. For example, the receiving, storage, preparation, production and warewashing areas and the non-production areas, such as rest rooms, lounges and offices, are brought together to form the basic floor plan for the facility.

There may be some question as to whether these two stages of layout are done at the same time. Even though the planner may be working on one stage or the other at any given moment, he must consider his layout decisions in terms of both stages. In essence, he must consider the layout of the total facility when he is laying out the component areas; and in turn, he must consider the layout of the component areas when he is laying out the total facility.

FLOW

The layout of food facilities is primarily guided by the basic concepts of flow. Depending on the situation, the flow of materials, employees, guests or paperwork may be evaluated in such a way as to minimize the movement required. The flow concepts may be used to arrive at equipment arrangements in functional areas as well as integrating functional areas into the total facility plan.

Most layout problems can be solved by evaluating the flow of a single variable. The layout of dishwashing areas for large operations, as illustrated in Fig. 11.1, can be based on the flow of dinnerware.

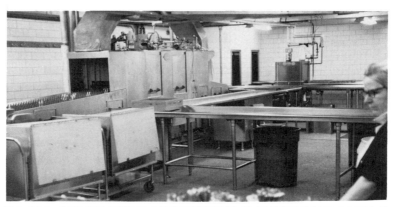

FIG. 11.1. ARRANGEMENT OF EQUIPMENT IN DISHWASHING AREAS IS BASED ON THE FLOW OF DINNERWARE

The location of the soiled-dish table, the dishwasher and the clean dish table will be based on minimizing the flow of the dinnerware. Another example of layout based on the flow of a single variable is the arrangement of short-order cooking areas which is so planned as to minimize the movements of the cook. In this case, the material flow is secondary to the efficiency of the employee. Serving facilities arranged to minimize the movements of people, both employees and guests, and office areas arranged to minimize the flow of paperwork are other examples of basing the layout on the flow of a single variable.

In some situations, the flow of two or more variables may be evaluated to determine the best layout. A salad preparation area may require evaluation of both the flow of foods and the movements of employees in order to arrive at the best layout. In most cases, arrangements that minimize the flow of materials are also those that minimize the movements of employees. This is likely when the materials are moved primarily by workers, but may not be the case if mechanical conveyors are used. If there is any doubt, both flows should be evaluated.

Regardless of the type of flow selected as the criterion for layout, the following principles can be applied:

(1) Flow should be along straight-line paths as much as possible.

(2) The amount of cross flow or cross traffic should be minimized.

(3) Backtracking should be minimized.

(4) Bypassing should be minimized.

These principles of flow, regardless of whether they are applied to the movement of materials or people, can be used for all types of layout problems. The concept of keeping flow in a straight line is the most important because it results in movements over the shortest distance. To utilize this concept, the designer will visualize or chart the flow involved with several different arrangements and select the one that gives the best straight-line pattern. Flow analyses for layout problems involving only a few pieces of equipment are easy to do. Layout problems involving numerous pieces of equipment or areas will require more extensive flow analysis. Some planners find flow diagrams or string charts a helpful tool in evaluating complex flow patterns.

With the great variety of materials and activities found in food service operations, the concept of minimizing cross traffic is important, because it results in layouts that are free of bottlenecks and congestion. This concept is especially pertinent to fast-food operations which have peak periods of flow. Cross traffic is minimized by the proper location of aisles, passageways and doors. Some cross traffic can be tolerated if it results in shorter flow patterns. However, if the cross traffic creates a hazardous situation, it should be eliminated, even at the cost of increased distance of movement. Cross traffic between employees and guests is undesirable and should be eliminated.

Backtracking occurs when a material or person moves from one piece of equipment or an area back to the point where the movement originated. The flow is back along the same path that was just traversed. Of course, many of the tasks required in food service operations involve a sequence of movements that make it practically impossible to eliminate all backtracking. Many of the cooking and production tasks are of this nature. In those situations, minimizing the amount of backtracking is all that can be done. This involves evaluating several different equipment or space arrangements to find the best one.

Bypassing is the result of a material or person passing one or more pieces of equipment to get to the next piece of equipment required in the sequence of movements. Several different arrangements of the equipment or areas may have to be evaluated to determine which one results in the least amount of bypassing. As with cross traffic, it is impossible to eliminate all bypassing except in the very simplest of layout problems.

The ultimate goal of layout is to develop arrangements of equipment and spaces for the food facility that have primarily straight-line flow paths with a minimum of cross traffic, backtracking and bypassing.

OTHER CRITERIA FOR LAYOUT

Although flow has been identified as the most important criterion of layout, other modifying considerations which may affect some layout decisions should be evaluated before the arrangement is finalized. These include the following items:

(1) *Efficient use of utilities.* All equipment requiring steam, for example, may be placed together to economize on installation and operating costs.

(2) *Efficient use of equipment.* Some individual pieces of equipment that will be used in two or more functional areas can be placed in central locations so they are easily accessible.

(3) *Efficient use of skilled labor.* This requires arrangements of equipment that will minimize the movements of skilled personnel. This may increase the movements of other employees or increase the movement of materials. The decision may be based on an economic analysis of different arrangements.

(4) *Safety.* Some layouts based on the concepts of flow alone may result in an arrangement of equipment that is hazardous. Placing a deep-fat fryer next to a sink creates a dangerous situation, and safety should over-ride flow in this case. Other hazardous arrangements may result when high-temperature equipment is placed adjacent to a traffic aisle or near entrances and exits. If another location is not feasible, sufficient guarding and shielding of the equipment is an alternative solution.

(5) *Efficient use of space.* Building configurations and shapes may require rearrangement of some layouts to make full use of available space.

(6) *Environmental factors of noise and odor.* Some pieces of equipment or areas may be isolated from flow paths if they are objectionable and cannot be modified to render them environmentally acceptable. Garbage-can washers, as shown in Fig. 11.2, or incinerators illustrate this situation.

FIG. 11.2. OBJECTIONABLE EQUIPMENT LIKE THIS
GARBAGE CAN WASHER MAY BE ISOLATED FOR EN-
VIRONMENTAL REASONS

These modifying criteria may result in arrangements that are more
expensive than those based on flow alone. They have to be used
however, to achieve many of the objectives of planning that were
identified.

LAYOUT CONFIGURATIONS

The arrangement of equipment and workplaces for functional
areas is usually in the form of a straight line or in combinations and
modifications of straight-line configurations. The basic patterns that
may be used include:

(1) *Single straight-line arrangement.* This is the simplest of designs, but it is limited in the number of pieces of equipment
or workplaces that can be arranged. The straight-line arrangement may be placed along a wall or take the form of an island.

(2) *Ell-shaped arrangement.* This is a modification of the straight-line arrangement to accommodate more equipment and work-places; it is sometimes used where linear space is limited. The ell-shaped configuration is very suitable for separating two major groups of equipment. One group of equipment would be placed on one leg of the ell, the other group forming the second leg. An ell-shaped arrangement is shown in Fig. 11.3.

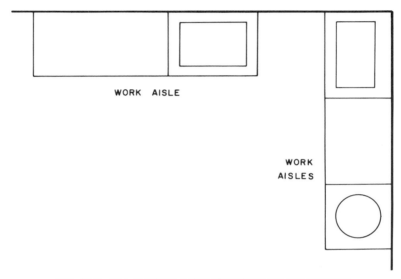

FIG. 11.3. ELL-SHAPED ARRANGEMENT OF EQUIPMENT

(3) *U-shaped arrangements.* The U-shaped configuration is ideal for small areas where only one or two employees are working. One disadvantage of this configuration is that straight-line flow through the area is not possible. A typical arrangement of equipment into the U-shape is shown in Fig. 11.4.

(4) *Parallel, back-to-back arrangement.* This configuration is an arrangement of two parallel lines where the backs of the equipment and/or workplaces on each line are adjacent to each other. This arrangement centralizes the utility lines required for equipment. Sometimes a short wall is placed between the two rows of equipment, in which case provision for cleaning and maintenance has to be allowed. Parallel, back-to-back arrangement of cooking equipment that must be vented is ideal because a single canopy hood can be used. The separation of major groups of equipment is easily accomplished with

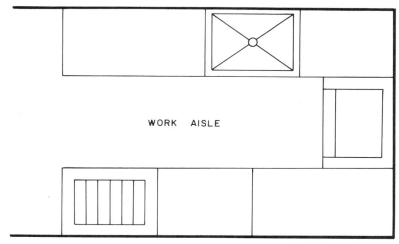

FIG. 11.4. U-SHAPED ARRANGEMENT OF EQUIPMENT

this configuration. Figure 11.5 illustrates parallel, back-to-back arrangement.

(5) *Parallel, face-to-face arrangement*. This arrangement utilizes two straight lines of equipment and/or workplaces where the fronts face each other and are separated by an aisle space. This is a very common configuration that can be used in many areas of the facility. A variation of this configuration is obtained by arranging a straight line of worktables between the

WORK AISLE

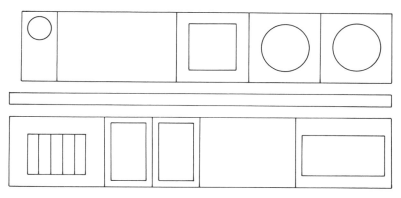

WORK AISLE

FIG. 11.5. PARALLEL, BACK-TO-BACK ARRANGEMENT OF EQUIPMENT

two rows of equipment. The parallel, face-to-face arrangement requires two separate utility lines for equipment, as compared to the single utility line used in the parallel, back-to-back arrangement.   Figure 11.6 shows the parallel, face-to-face arrangement.

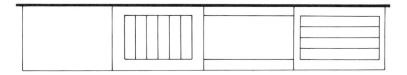

WORK   AISLE

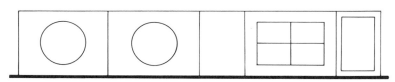

FIG. 11.6. PARALLEL, FACE-TO-FACE ARRANGEMENT OF EQUIPMENT

Modifications of any of the above-mentioned configurations can be used to handle special cases and problems. Tee-shaped, open-square or other configurations should be used if they result in the best solution to the layout problem.

Curved or circular configurations are sometimes used, but they should be planned very carefully to fit straight-line configurations that may be used in the facility. Circular serving islands for shopping-center cafeterias and curved cafeteria counters are examples of these configurations.

The final arrangement for most facilities is usually composed of a combination of configurations of equipment and workplaces. Only the smallest of operations would use a single configuration for the layout of the facility.

LAYOUT GUIDES

The basic concepts of flow along with the modifying considerations give the planner his basic guides for laying out the facility. It is not possible to discuss the layout of all areas for all types of food facilities, but general guides to the arrangement of some areas common to most facilities will be given.

Overall design of the facility is usually based on the flow of major food items. Since most food items are received and then stored before preparation, the dry, refrigerated and freezer storage areas should be adjacent to receiving areas and also be readily accessible to the various preparation areas. The main cooking area is so located as to receive the flow from the preparation areas and have an outlet directly to the serving area. The salad and sandwich preparation areas may be so placed that their flow of foods is directly into the serving area. Placement of the dining area adjacent to the serving area is obvious.

The flow of non-food items is next evaluated to locate other areas. The flow of dinnerware in a repetitive route from serving areas to dining areas and then back to serving areas requires the dishwashing area to be adjacent to both. Similarly, the flow of utensils dictates placing the pot- and pan-washing section near the main cooking, baking and serving areas.

Areas involving the flow of people are then blended into the layout in a manner that does not interfere with the flow of materials. Thus the overall layout of the facility by functional areas begins to take shape.

LAYOUT OF STORAGE AREAS

The layout of storage areas is based on convenience and accessibility. Arrangements that allow heavy and bulky materials to be moved as little and as easily as possible are preferred. Central storage facilities with several satellite locations are good arrangements for many types of facilities. The storage space in the preparation, processing and other functional areas should be planned so they do not interfere with efficient work methods. The use of combination walk-in and reach-in storage units may increase the convenience of these areas.

It is best to plan walk-in storage areas in a manner which keeps the products at least 8 in. above the floor to facilitate cleaning. An alternative would be to use mobile bins and containers that can be easily moved when the area is cleaned.

Storage areas for non-food supplies may be located in the various functional areas as required. Storage space for china, glass and silverware may be provided in serving or dining areas. Linen and paper goods used for service are also stored in or near these areas.

LAYOUT OF MAIN COOKING AREA

Laying out the main cooking area is the key to fast and efficient production of foods. The flow patterns affecting this area include inflow of foods from storage and preparation areas and utensils from the pot- and pan-washing area. Outflow of foods to the serving, salad preparation and sandwich preparation areas is common. The cooking equipment should be arranged so that the most frequently used pieces are close to the pick-up location.

Other factors related to the design of the main cooking area include the following:

(1) All heat- and moisture-producing equipment, such as fryers, broilers, griddles, ranges and steamers, should be placed under ventilating hoods or be equipped with individual venting systems.

(2) Steam cooking equipment requires special installation including depressed floors or the use of curbs.

(3) Some types of equipment require air for ventilation or cooling of enclosed spaces; vents and grill openings should not be blocked by other pieces of equipment.

(4) Provision has to be made to permit venting of fuel-burning equipment directly to the outside.

(5) Location of the main building ventilation or air-conditioning inlets is important to effect adequate cooling of the air without cooling the cooking equipment or interfering with the equipment venting system.

(6) If remote banquet rooms are to be served, methods of transporting hot foods and appropriate space for loading have to be considered.

(7) The use of partially or fully pre-processed foods will increase the need for refrigerated space in the cooking areas.

LAYOUT OF PREPARATION AREAS

The layout of preparation areas is fairly easy because most of the functions performed in them follow a logical sequence, and thus the equipment is arranged in the same sequence. Vegetable preparation, for example, basically involves trimming, washing and size reduction, in that order. A straight-line arrangement of a work table for trimming, a sink for washing and draining, and equipment for size reduction becomes the layout for the area. Since the inflow of vegetables is from storage areas, the trimming table is placed close to them; consequently, the size-reduction equipment is placed near the main cooking and salad preparation areas. Provision for temporary storage of materials and removal of waste will complete the layout of the vegetable preparation area for a small facility. Larger operations will require more space and equipment and take longer to lay out.

Salad preparation areas are planned in a similar manner. The foods should flow in a continuous path from the start of the preparation tasks, through the various workplaces and equipment, which are arranged in the order of the steps required, and on to the serving area. Operations that prepare a large number of the same or very similar salads may be designed by the concepts of mass assembly.

LAYOUT OF SERVING AREAS

The layout of serving areas is based on the method and speed of service desired. Serving equipment should be arranged in the order of use, and should be located so they are easily accessible to serving personnel.

Table Service

Hot food pick-up areas are located adjacent to the main cooking battery. Provisions for maintaining the temperature of hot foods at pick-up areas should be considered. Additional serving stations or pantries for salads, desserts, rolls and beverages are located nearer the dining area to avoid congestion. Linen, flatware, water and butter used for setups are best placed in inconspicuous areas of the dining room. These stations may also include facilities for depositing soiled linen and tableware.

Counter Service

Most of the cooking and serving facilities in typical counter-service operations occur at the back bar opposite the dining counter. A common layout is to have a straight-line back bar with straight-line or a series of U-shaped dining counters. Some operations offering a more extensive menu may require additional preparation and cooking facilities that can be located in a separate area. An efficient layout in this case is to have the pick-up counter as a part of the back bar. This is also a good arrangement for operations having both counter and table-service sections. The pick-up area should be located for easy access to the table servers.

Cafeteria Service

Cafeteria counters are placed as close to the production areas as possible with due regard to the free flow of customers or users. The layout of cafeteria counters is based on the shape of the serving area and the anticipated traffic patterns. Counters may be arranged in a straight line, ell-shaped, U-shaped, hollow square or combinations of these configurations, as dictated by the length of counter required.

The design of the counter should allow displayed foods that are usually selected in combination to be placed together on the counter. Merchandising concepts call for desserts and salads to be located at the beginning of the line; hot foods should be at the end of the line to minimize cooling. Special care is needed in providing for cashiering, since this is one of the bottleneck areas in commercial cafeterias.

The entire design of the cafeteria service system is based on volume flow, and anything that will speed service should be incorporated into the layout. Silver, napkins, water and condiments may be located in stations away from the main counter area. Islands placed between the serving and dining areas are frequently used for this purpose. Self-dispensing equipment for beverages will also help speed the flow of people.

Cook-to-order items cause delays and are best located in a separate area where patrons can pull out of the main stream of flow to wait for their orders. This can be easily accomplished with the open square arrangement of counters.

LAYOUT OF DISHWASHING AREAS

The layout of dishwashing areas should follow the sequence of operations performed in washing. The arrangement has to provide for sorting, scraping or pre-flushing and stacking, prior to loading the dishwashing machine. If glasses and silverware are to be washed separately, provisions for these operations have to be planned.

Pre-flushing of soiled dishes may be accomplished in one of two ways. One method is to use a continuous flow of water over the dishes as they are being scraped. A disposal unit is used to handle the food wastes. The other method uses an overhead spray and is suitable for dishes that are placed in dish racks. In either case, the soiled-dish table has to be designed so that water is quickly drained away. Raised edges on the table help prevent excess water spillage.

Regardless of the type of dishwashing machine used, space for loading and unloading must be arranged. Rack-type machines are frequently loaded in a straight-line flow from the soiled-dish table. Rackless or peg-type machines require space for the loader to handle the individual pieces of dinnerware.

Clean-dish areas are arranged so adequate drying time is allowed before the removal and stacking of dinnerware takes place. The flow of dinnerware through the dishwashing area is planned to be continuous and over the shortest possible distance.

The layout of other areas for the food facility should be accomplished in the same manner as given in the above examples. When all the preceding steps of the planning process are satisfactorily completed, the layout step becomes fairly easy. The final layout reflects the amount of time and care taken in completing the other steps of the planning process.

BIBLIOGRAPHY

AVERY, A. C. 1968. Simplified food service layout. Cornell Hotel, Restaurant Admin. Quart. *9*, No. 1, 114–119.

BANGS, O. E. 1968. A master plan for food service design. Kitchen Planning *5*, No. 1, 19–21.

FISK, M., HART, K., and MILLER, G. 1963. Long range planning for food service layouts. J. Am. Dietet. Assoc. *42*, No. 6, 489–495.

KAZARIAN, E. A. 1969. Work Analysis and Design for Hotels, Restaurants and Institutions, Avi Publishing Co., Westport, Conn.

SCHNEIDER, N. F., JOHN, E. A., and SMITH, A. Q. 1962. Commercial Kitchens. American Gas Assoc., New York.

CHAPTER 12

Example Food Service Layouts

INTRODUCTION

The planning of food service facilities involves developing layouts for a wide variety of operations. Each layout should reflect the type of menu entrees to be prepared, the production processes to be used, the equipment choices and the method of operation desired by management. This chapter presents illustrations of layouts for several different types of food service operations. The plans shown are examples and are not intended to represent the only layout suitable for each type of operation.

Grateful acknowledgment is made to *Kitchen Planning Magazine* for permission to reproduce the plans and descriptions of the food service facilities shown.

GENERAL RESTAURANTS

Howard Johnson

A prototype of the Howard Johnson's roadside restaurants is shown in Fig. 12.1. The kitchen was planned to prepare the chain's own frozen products and was developed on the concept of minimum on-the-site food preparation. This design concept has reduced the total kitchen areas by about 50% from their earlier designs. This was primarily accomplished by reducing the space required for food storage, dishwashing and potwashing. The meat and vegetable preparation areas were eliminated to save space. A reduction in the baking area over older designs was also included in the new design.

The kitchen layout uses modern reconstituting equipment, including convection ovens and microwave ovens for heating frozen foods. All cooking equipment is located so that a cook can reach it by pivoting or walking a short distance. The range, charbroiler, fryers and griddle are also conveniently located adjacent to the pick-up area. When orders are prepared, they are placed on a pass shelf directly in front of the cook's station.

The kitchen is supported by a pantry located directly off the dining room and adjacent to the kitchen. A pass-through shelf is placed between the kitchen and the pantry thus providing more pick-up area for the waitresses. The pantry contains all the necessary equipment for coffee, rolls, pastry, cocktails, etc., eliminating the need for

EQUIPMENT
KEY
1. Ice machine
2. Mixer
3. Work Table
4. Slicer
5. Work Table/Sink
6. Dishwasher
7. Pot sink
8. Proof Cabinet
9. Oven
10. Refrigerator
11. Range
12. Charbroiler
13. Fryers
14. Salad table
15. Clam table
16. Steam table
17. Oven
18. Griddle
19. Toaster
20. Milk dispenser
21. Soft shake machine
22. Multimixer
23. Ice cream cabinet
24. Milk dispenser
25. Roll warmer
26. Drink dispenser
27. Coffee urn

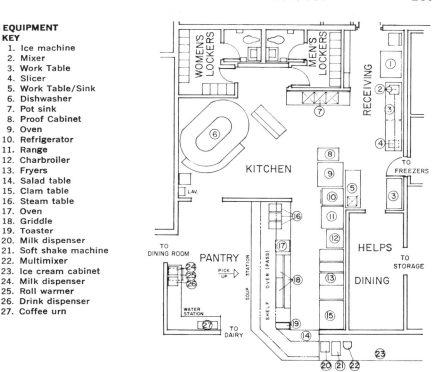

FIG. 12.1. KITCHEN FACILITIES FOR A HOWARD JOHNSON'S RESTAURANT

waitresses to enter the kitchen directly. Milk, ice cream and soda fountain items are also easily accessible to the waitresses.

This design reflects the minimum space and equipment required for a food service facility using primarily convenience foods.

Red Fox

The kitchen facilities for the Machus Red Fox restaurant in West Bloomfield, Michigan (Fig. 12.2) are geared to preparing high-quality meals. The restaurant was designed to appeal to suburbanites who are in a high income bracket and would generate a moderately high check average. The menu offers popular items which can be rapidly prepared and served.

Some of the basic planning objectives for this food service facility were:

(1) design for a minimum number of employees;
(2) kitchen and support facilities located as close to the point of service as possible;
(3) minimum distance travelled by waitresses in serving guests.

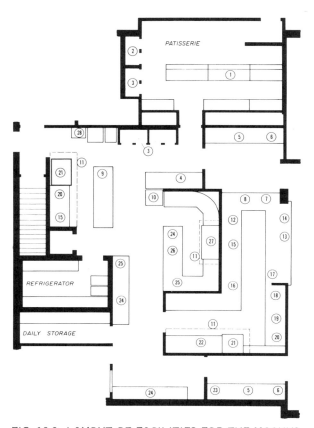

FIG. 12.2. LAYOUT OF FACILITIES FOR THE MACHUS
RED FOX RESTAURANT

1—Display and wrapping counter, 2—Freezer, 3—Refrigerator,
4—Ice-cream cabinet, 5—Coffee maker, 6—Water and ice bin,
7—Dressing inserts, 8—Salad crisper, 9—Work table, 10—
Mixer, 11—Hood, 12—Salamander, 13—Heat lamps, 14—Order
holder, 15—Broiler, 16—Slicer, 17—Roll warmer, 18—Fryer,
19—Griddle, 20—Range, 21—Oven, 22—Broaster, 23—Milk
dispenser, 24—Sinks, 25—Disposer, 26—Soiled dish table,
27—Dishwasher, 28—Bread rack.

The cook-to-order menu items are prepared in an area adjacent to
the dining room and include a salamander, broiler, fryer, griddle,
range, oven and broaster. Adequate worktable space and a slicer are
also in this area. Orders are prepared and then placed directly on the
pick-up counter for the waitresses. Additional items can be prepared
at either the range, broiler or oven located at the left side of the
kitchen.

Pantry areas are duplicated on either side of the cook-to-order area so waitresses can minimize the distance travelled for coffee, water, and ice.

Spanish Oaks

The kitchen layout for the Spanish Oaks, a specialty restuarant serving Spanish foods, is shown in Fig. 12.3.

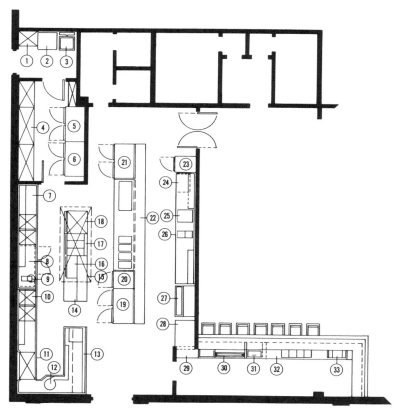

FIG. 12.3. KITCHEN FACILITIES FOR THE SPANISH OAKS RESTAURANT

1—Shelving, 2—Receiving table, 3—Scale, 4—Shelving, 5—Freezer,[1] 6—Refrigerator,[1] 7—Preparation table and sinks, 8—Undercounter refrigerator, 9—Mixer, 10—Pot sinks, 11—Dishwasher, 12—Disposer, 13—Dishtables, 14—Worktable,[1] 15—Exhaust hood, 16—Broiler, 17—Range, 18—Oven, 19—Refrigerator, 20—Freezer, 21—Refrigerator, 22—Chef's counter, 23—Refrigerator, 24—Roll warmer, 25—Coffee maker, 26—Service stand, 27—Ice machine, 28—Drink table, 29—Pass-through shelf, 30—Beer dispenser, 31—Glass chiller, 32—Sinks, 33—Cocktail unit.

[1] Numbers 5 and 6 are for future expansion, and number 14 is designed for the addition of another oven.

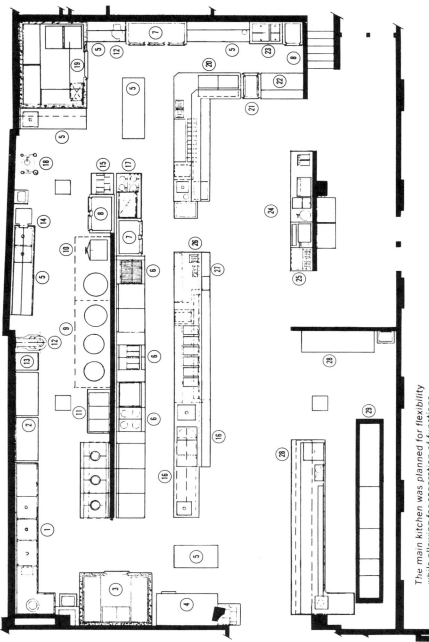

The main kitchen was planned for flexibility while allowing for separation of functions.

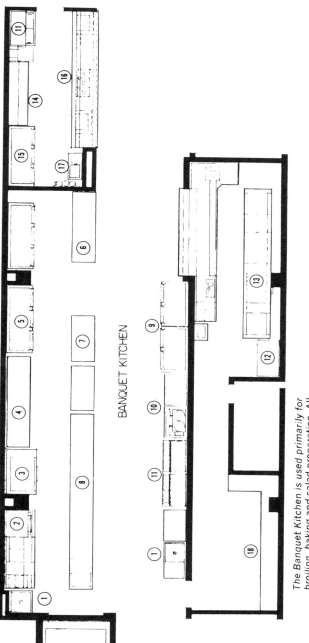

BANQUET KITCHEN

The Banquet Kitchen is used primarily for broiling, baking and salad preparation. All soups, gravies and vegetables are prepared in the main kitchen.

FIG. 12.4. MAIN KITCHEN (UPPER) AND BANQUET KITCHEN (LOWER) FOR THE ROYAL SONESTA HOTEL

Upper: 1—Potwash sink, 2—Racks, 3—Cook's refrigerator, 4—Oven, 5—Table, 6—Ranges, 7—Refrigerator, 8—Freezer, 9—Kettles, 10—Steamer, 11—Bain marie, 12—Mixer, 13—Mixer accessory rack, 14—Vegetable sink and peeler, 15—Slicer on portable stand, 16—Combination cook's table, 17—Waffle bakers, 18—V/C mixer, 19—Salad refrigerator, 20—Pantry counter, 21—Pass-through refrigerator, 22—Pastry pick-up, 23—Ice-cream cabinet, 24—Beverage stand, 25—Toasters, 26—Storage, 27—Egg boiler, 28—Tray ledge, 29—Dishwasher.

Lower: 1—Sink, 2—Fryer, broiler, 3—Oven, 4—Food warmers, 5—Roll-in refrigerators, 6—Worktable, 7—Portable hot-food carts, 8—Hot table, 9—Freezers, 10—Coffee center, 11—Ice makers, 12—Soiled-dish table, 13—Flight dishwasher, 14—Back bar, 15—Refrigerator, 16—Mix station, 17—Soda system, 18—Storage.

The menu for Spanish Oaks includes 20 entrees with a complimentary house relish tray. Entrees include a choice of baked or parsley potatoes and a vegetable of the day. A wide selection of soups, salads and desserts is also available.

The kitchen was planned for the basic roasting and sautéing requirements of the predominantly Spanish menu. The chef's area is centrally located with everything within easy reach. As most entree items are cooked to order, there is a minimum of steam-table and other food-holding equipment.

Future expansion of kitchen space is provided in anticipation of increased sales volume. Space has been provided for an additional oven, another freezer and another refrigerator. These items can be quickly moved into place and installed without major alterations to the structure. The dishwashing and potwashing areas were planned for current needs and any envisioned expansion, since these facilities are more difficult to expand after they have been installed.

The dining area seats 85 customers with room for 40 more in the cocktail lounge. The facility was designed so that a dining-room wall could be easily removed to incorporate additional dining space in an adjacent building.

HOTEL FOOD SERVICE

Royal Sonesta Hotel

Food service facilities for hotels have to be planned to accommodate not only the variety of in-house restaurants but a large volume of banquet business as well. Since banquets require peak production, an auxiliary kitchen is frequently used to prepare some of the items. An example of kitchen facilities for hotel food service is shown in Fig. 12.4. These facilities are in the Royal Sonesta Hotel in New Orleans.

The variety of food service facilities at the hotel include a main dining room which is a complex of three rooms—a bar, a restaurant and a gallery which overlooks a central patio. The main dining room features a varied Creole cuisine and thus the kitchen facilities were planned to prepare the unusual specialties. The oyster bar features seafood delicacies, such as fresh oysters, shrimp, crawfish and crabs. The garden patio features indoor and outdoor service for breakfast and luncheon. Two smaller rooms adjacent to the main dining room are used for private parties.

The convention and meeting facilities for the hotel include a Grand Ballroom which can accommodate 600 persons and a number of smaller rooms with capacities of from 40 to 75 persons.

The hotel has two kitchens—the main kitchen and a smaller banquet kitchen. The banquet kitchen is used primarily for broiling, baking and salad preparation for the banquets. All soups, gravies and vegetables are prepared in the main kitchen. Major cooking equipment, including steam kettles and pressure cookers, are located in the main kitchen.

The main kitchen was planned for flexibility while allowing for separation of functions. During slow periods, it is easy for kitchen employees to double on different stations.

The main cooking area is arranged in a straight line with a combination cook's table which has undercounter hot and cold storage, plate warmers and the bain marie. The cooking section is backed by a preparation area which includes another bain marie, ranges, kettles, steamers and a freezer. Across the aisle are the pot-washing facilities, a mixer and the vegetable preparation area.

The pantry and salad preparation areas are at the far end of the kitchen in a side-by-side arrangement. An ell-shaped pantry counter allows for working on one side and serving on the other. At the other end of this area is a dessert service station.

The banquet kitchen has a straight-line arrangement of cooking facilities, including a fryer, range, broiler and oven, as well as the essential and extensive equipment for holding hot and cold foods. This kitchen is capable of storing 1000 prepared plates for banquets. The kitchen has its own dishwashing facility to handle all the dinnerware used for banquet service. There is also a complete service bar for serving drinks.

The Greenery

The Greenery is a quick-service coffee shop type of hotel food service facility located in the Hotel Ambassador in Chicago. The kitchen facilities for this restaurant are shown in Fig. 12.5. The coffee shop was developed by converting a linen storage area after the hotel was built. All electric equipment was planned to minimize the venting requirements. The equipment was selected for preparing and serving short-order foods typically found on coffee shop menus. The basic cooking equipment consists of one electric broiler, two griddles, one friolator and one steam table.

The Greenery has both booths and tables with a seating capacity for 60 persons and can handle up to 6 turnovers for breakfast. The 7-day-a-week food service operation uses two short-order cooks for all three meal periods. Much of the equipment selected for the facility is of a self-service type, including the soda fountain. This aids the quick preparation and service required to achieve a high turnover.

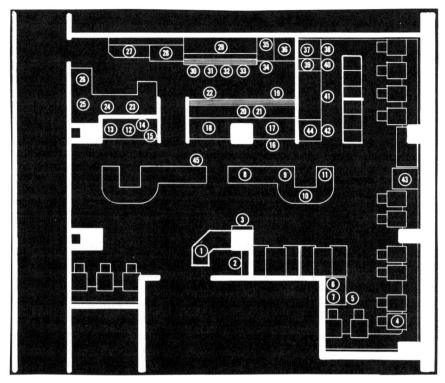

FIG. 12.5. LAYOUT OF FACILITIES FOR THE GREENERY

1—Cashier's stand and register, 2—Cigarette rack, 3—Newspaper rack, 4—Tables, chairs and booths, 5—Service stand, 6—Coffee warmer, 7—Water and ice station, 8—Counter and stools, 9—Coffee warmer, 10—Ice bin, 11—Water station, 12—Utility stand, 13—Coffee urn, 14—Cream dispenser, 15—Iced-tea dispenser, 16—Serving counter, 17—Refrigerated dessert section, 18—Refrigerator and pastry section, 19—Salad and sandwich table, 20—Bread and muffin toasters, 21—Egg boilers, 22—Hot-food table, 23—Dish tables, 24—Disposer, 25—Dishwasher, 26—Hot-water booster, 27—Worktable, 28—Refrigerated base, 29—Equipment stand, 30—Fryer, 31—Hot plate, 32—Griddle (20-in.), 33—Griddle (36-in.), 34—Utility table, 35—Waffle baker, 36—Refrigerator, 37—Milk dispenser, 38—Table, 39—Malt mixer, 40—Sink and dipper well, 41—Soda fountain, 42—Table, 43—Plate lowerators, 44—Roll warmer, 45—Undercounter sink.

FAST FOOD

The fast food facility shown in Fig. 12.6 represents the standard design for Bonanza International. The design was based on being able to produce limited-menu items that are uniform in quality and taste for all units in the organization. The operation concentrates on steaks and baked potatoes.

The facility is designed with a serving counter capable of serving

EQUIPMENT KEY

1. Tray/silver stand
2. Pastry cabinet
3. Salad unit
4. Refrigerator
5. Glass dispenser
6. Ice dispenser

7. Drink dispenser
8. Coffee maker
9. Cup dispenser
10. Hot food unit
11. Cashier stand
12. Oven

13. Fryer
14. Plate dispenser
15. Griddle
16. Broiler
17. Syrup rack
18. Table

19. Hot plate
20. Dishwasher
21. Mixer
22. Disposer
23. Sink
24. Pot washer

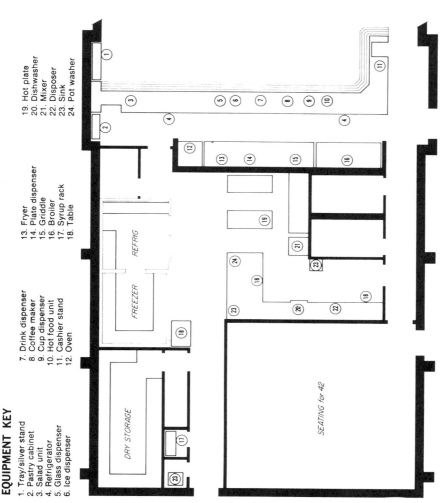

FIG. 12.6. STANDARD DESIGN OF FACILITIES FOR BONANZA INTERNATIONAL

175 persons per hour under normal operating conditions, with a maximum rate of 225 persons per hour when two or three additional employees are used. The basic serving counter is 40 ft long. Staffing for the serving line includes:

(1) an order taker who also helps with salads and desserts;
(2) a person for make-up including potato and butter preparation, garnish, Texas toast and hamburgers;
(3) a fryer for french fries, shrimp and chicken;
(4) a broilerman for the steaks;
(5) a beverage server;
(6) a cashier.

The back bar cooking equipment for the facility includes an oven, fryers, griddle and a broiler.

The overall design for the operation was based on minimum movement of materials from receiving to service. Minimum employee movements were also a basic objective of the design. The floor plan shown allows for a private dining room with a seating capacity for 42 persons. This is an allowable variation of the standard kitchen design.

COLLEGE FOOD SERVICE

The planning of college or university food service facilities involves careful consideration of future needs if the facility is to handle increasing student enrollments. The food service operation shown in Fig. 12.7 illustrates this type of planning project. Future needs were anticipated and appropriate allowances were made for additional space and equipment.

The present facility combines a cafeteria on one side and a snack bar unit on the other. Each component has a seating capacity of 300 people. A private dining area is adjacent to the snack bar. Both units are serviced by a single 6200 sq ft kitchen. For lunch, the cafeteria currently serves about 600 students and the snack bar serves about 900 students, for a total of 1500.

The dining schedules for the cafeteria and snack bar are arranged to complement each other. Only the cafeteria is open from 7:00 a.m. to 8:30 a.m. for breakfast. The snack bar is then opened at 8:30 a.m. and both units are used for the luncheon surge. The snack bar closes at 4:30 p.m. when the cafeteria opens for the evening meal. Then, when the cafeteria closes at 7:30 p.m., the snack bar is reopened to handle the late evening snacks. This scheduling of the units allows management to adjust the dining capacity of the facility as needed.

The cafeteria offers a multiple-selection menu with a minimum of three entrees.   A great deal of the preparation, including baking, salads and meat preparation, is done the day before and the food kept under refrigeration.

The snack bar offers the standard hamburgers, hot dogs, sandwiches, beverages and other typical snack items.

The cafeteria unit is designed so that students can pick up condiments, trays, sugar and napkins at a station in the dining area.   The cafeteria line includes sections for hot foods, salads, desserts, beverages and coffee, in that order.   The cashier is stationed at the end of the line in the dining area.   At the back of the cafeteria line are the facilities for holding hot foods, cold foods and desserts.   Equipment in this area includes a two-section hot food pass-through unit and a three-section refrigerator.   Both units can accommodate roll-racks which take standard 18 by 26-in. pans.   The panned food is racked into the portable units and rolled into the holding units for replenishing the cafeteria line.

The kitchen plan features a double-doored receiving dock with openings to the receiving area and to the facilities for storing and washing trash cans.   Three walk-in refrigerators for food storage are located next to the receiving area and also close to the vegetable preparation area.   The vegetable preparation area includes a sink unit with disposals, two salad preparation tables, a potato peeler and a cutter-mixer unit.

The meat and vegetable cooking areas are arranged back-to-back with a divider wall between them which houses the ventilation system.

The equipment for the vegetable-cooking section includes two 40-gal. and one 60-gal. kettle.   Space for another 60-gal. kettle has been reserved for future installation.   The vegetable section also has a 60-qt mixer and two portable worktables.

The meat-cooking area includes a double-deck convection oven, two deep-fat fryers, a griddle, broiler, and range.   This area is located conveniently to both the cafeteria and the snack bar.   Provisions for installing additional equipment in this area were also planned for.

The back bar in the snack unit includes a sandwich work area, soft ice-cream machine, a fry station, food warmer and griddle.   Space for additional equipment to be installed in the future has been allotted.

The snack bar is primarily self-service and the counter has a hot-food warmer with compartments for soup, sandwiches and a single entree.   A cold pan for salads and desserts and self-service beverage dispensers for juice, carbonated drinks, coffee and hot choclate are also on the counter.   The snack bar is 100% paper service, and a paper goods storeroom is located behind the service area.

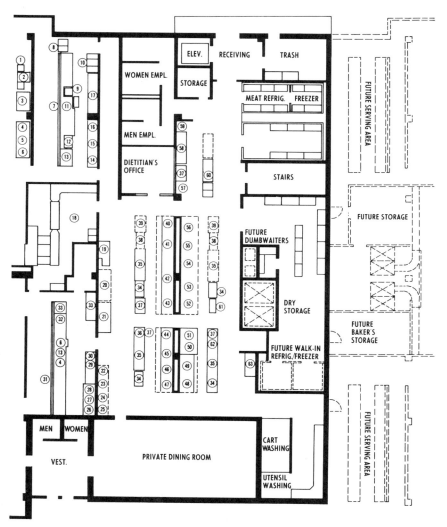

FIG. 12.7. TYPICAL LAYOUT FOR COLLEGE FOOD SERVICE FACILITIES

Key to Fig. 12.7.

1—Cream dispenser	34—Even heat range with oven
2—Mobile undercounter coffee urn	35—Fry top range with oven
3—Hot beverage and cashier's stand	36—Double-deck roast oven
4—Mobile cup and saucer dispenser	37—Mobile parts cabinet
5—Mobile milk dispenser	38—60-qt mixer
6—Paper cup dispenser	39—80-qt mixer
7—Iced-tea urn	40—Hi-pressure steam cooker and freezer
8—Display shelf/cold pan	41—Counter refrigerator
9—Mobile undercounter shelf unit	42—Tilting electric skillet
10—Refrigerated cold pan	43—Mobile angle ledge racks
11—Sandwich, salad, dessert-serving table	44—Electric slicer with mobile stand
12—Butter chip dispenser	45—Mobile supply cabinet
13—Mobile china dispenser	46—Mobile table racks
14—Soup cup racks	47—Bain marie
15—Infrared warmers	48—Griddle
16—Hot-food table	49—Mobile table
17—Hot-food wells	50—80-gal. steam kettle ($^2/_3$ jacket)
18—Elevated pass-through food warmer	51—80-gal. steam kettle (full jacket)
19—Table	52—60-gal. steam kettle with agitator
20—Hot-bread well	53—3-compartment steamer
21—Salad and dessert racks	54—Vertical cutter mixer
22—Roll-through refrigerator	55—40-qt tilting kettle with table
23—Mobile dessert cabinet	56—Revolving bowl cutter with mobile stand
24—Mobile ice-cream cabinet	57—Sink
25—Scoop vat and faucet	58—Mobile pan shelving
26—Table with sink	59—Mixing bowls with mobile stand
27—Mobile ice dispenser	60—Mobile scale
28—Mobile tray dispenser	61—Can opener
29—Elevated broilers	62—Reach-in refrigerator
30—Double deck back shelf	63—Mobile root vegetable shelving
31—Double deck infrared gas broiler	64—Vegetable peeler
32—Convection oven	65—Vegetable tank carts
33—Oven top range with oven	

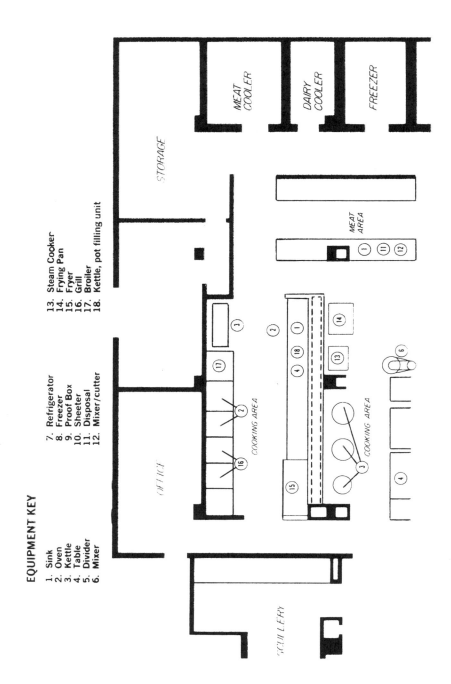

EQUIPMENT KEY

1. Sink
2. Oven
3. Kettle
4. Table
5. Divider
6. Mixer

7. Refrigerator
8. Freezer
9. Proof Box
10. Sheeter
11. Disposal
12. Mixer/cutter

13. Steam Cooker
14. Frying Pan
15. Fryer
16. Grill
17. Broiler
18. Kettle, pot filling unit

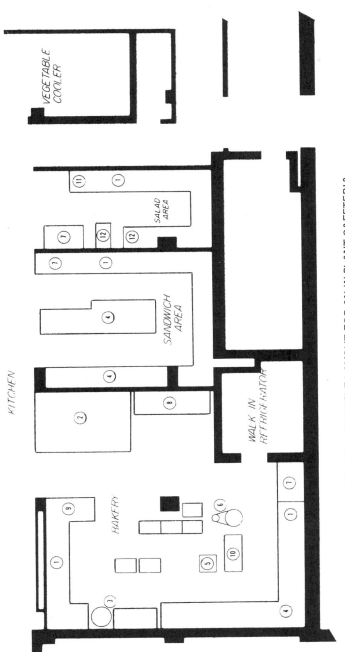

FIG. 12.8. EXAMPLE LAYOUT FOR AN IN-PLANT CAFETERIA

The proposed expansion of the food service facility is indicated by the dotted lines on the plan.

IN-PLANT CAFETERIA

Figure 12.8 shows the kitchen layout for an in-plant cafeteria which has a seating capacity of 586. The cafeteria feeds an average of 2750 people per day during three meal periods; 1800 at midday; 350 at mid-afternoon; and 600 in the evening.

The cafeteria uses the same menu for all three meal periods. The menu offers two hot main dishes and several types of hot sandwiches. Eight other types of sandwiches are offered to diners who do not want a hot lunch. Desserts include a choice of two pies, a pastry, ice cream, gelatin dessert and fresh fruit.

The kitchen plan features 5 walk-in refrigerators and 3 walk-in freezers for food storage. A large rotary oven is used for baking and roasting. Roller carts are used extensively to bring food trays from ovens and freezers to the serving area, where they are placed in 9 pass-through warming cabinets or refrigerators located directly in back of the serving stations.

Other basic kitchen equipment includes 4 deep-fat fryers, 3 grills, 3 50-gal. steam-jacketed kettles, a 3-tier pressure cooker, a bain marie, and 3 slicers. The salad and sandwich areas are provided with ample work surface space.

All baking for the cafeteria is done on the premises. Other than the rotary oven, the bakery equipment includes a proofer, 6 stainless steel flour bins, a 35-gal. steam-jacketed kettle, a deep fryer for donuts, 2 mixers, a dough sheeter and refrigerated storage.

The equipment layout uses a variety of configurations, including the back-to-back, face-to-face, ell- and U-shaped. The kitchen layout is primarily based on straightline flow of materials.

HOSPITAL FOOD SERVICE

The special dietary considerations for hospitals require a wide variety of equipment, as shown in Fig. 12.9. This hospital allows the patient to choose one or more of 19 entrees, 6 cold salads and 5 sandwiches for lunch and dinner. As food orders are placed one day in advance, adequate time exists for checking dietary requirements as well as planning the food production for the following day.

When the meals are prepared, they are placed in sealed trays to reduce heat loss. The meals are then conveyed from the kitchen to the patients' floors in specially designed electric cart lifts. On arrival at the designated floor, the lift doors open and an automatic ejector unloads the cart without manual handling. The meals are then rolled to the rooms and served to the patients.

A typical day's production for the hospital includes 700 regular and specially prepared meals and 300 meals for the employee and guest cafeteria.

Basic equipment in the kitchen includes an ice machine, food cutter and slicer, pellet heater, two convection ovens, a steamer, griddle top range, two hot top ranges, a trunnion kettle, a microwave oven, a bain marie and a conveyor line for the tray makeup. Additional equipment is identified in the equipment key.

AIRLINE FEEDING

An airline catering kitchen has to be planned for the timely production of large quantities of food. The kitchen shown in Fig. 12.10 is capable of turning out 7500 meals per day for airline passengers as well as providing meals for up to 5000 diners in the air terminal's dining room, coffee shop, snack bar and employee cafeteria. The production of meals is accelerated by (1) use of prefabricated foods, (2) the division of labor so employees become highly efficient, and (3) the use of moving-belt assembly lines.

The problems of preparing and timing meals for many different planes are numerous and complex. A highly sophisticated communications system between the various airlines and the commissary is required to make sure that the right number of meals are prepared in time and placed aboard the departing planes. Usually, three basic messages are relayed from the airlines to the commissary. The first two preliminary messages give flight information, such as flight number, size of plane, number of first and second class seats, what time the plane should land and what time it should depart. The menu for the flight is also checked. The third message, one hour before the plane is scheduled to depart, relays the number of passengers and the section they will occupy. This message starts the production of the meals for the plane.

Frozen entrees and other items are put on to cook. An assembly line for hot foods is used to fill the plastic dishes and to package them into containers which are then placed in a hot-food holding unit. Meanwhile, employees are placing salads, appetizers, desserts and silverware on individual plastic trays on the cold-food assembly line. Each tray that is made up is put in a chilled unit ready to be placed aboard the plane.

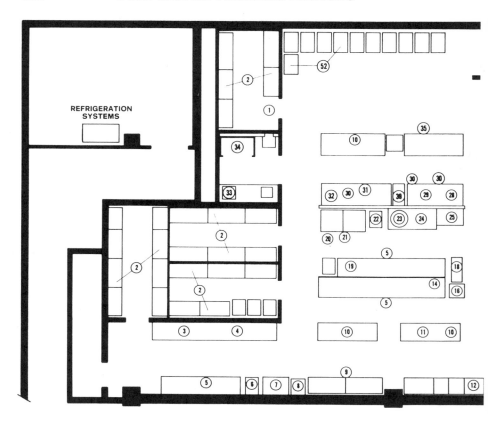

EQUIPMENT KEY

Century City Hospital

1. Cold storage rooms
2. Shelving
3. Preparation sink
4. Disposer
5. Counter
6. Racks
7. Ice bin
8. Flake ice machine
9. Pot racks
10. Table
11. Food chopper
12. Pot sink assembly
13. Underliner dispenser

14. Toaster
15. Pellet heater
16. Mixer parts cabinet
17. Plate dispenser
18. Mixer
19. Slicer
20. Ventilator exhaust
21. Convection ovens
22. Undercounter refrigerator
23. Kettle
24. Steamers
25. Heated cabinets
26. Cover dispenser

FIG. 12.9. EXAMPLE LAYOUT OF FACILITIES FOR HOSPITAL FOOD SERVICE

27. Hot food units
28. Broiler
29. Griddle top range
30. Spreader
31. Hot top ranges
32. Trunnion kettle
33. Electronic oven
34. Freezer
35. Table w/bain marie
36. Coffee urn
37. Cup & saucer dispenser
38. Toaster
39. Fryers

40. Ice cream cabinet
41. Milk dispenser
42. Mobile carts
43. Refrigerator
44. Starter station
45. Roll-in refrigerator
46. Cash register
47. Cream dispenser
48. Hood
49. Drink dispenser
50. Heat lamps
51. Tray & silver dispenser
52: Cart

FIG. 12.10. EXAMPLE LAYOUT FOR AIRLINE FEEDING

EQUIPMENT KEY

1. Refrigerator
2. Work table
3. Mixer
4. Food cutter
5. Toasters
6. Freezers
7. Kettle
8. Steamer

9. Fryer
10. Convection oven
11. Food warmer
12. Bain marie
13. Cold food assembly
    table
14. Hot food assembly
    table

15. Ranges
16. Char broiler
17. Pan rack
18. Baker's stove
19. Dough divider
20. Oven
21. Proof box
22. Baker racks

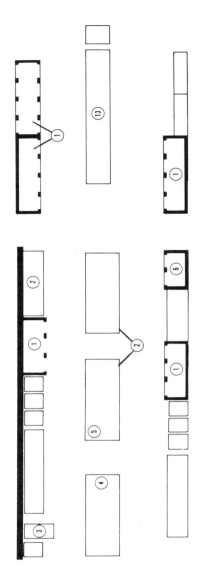

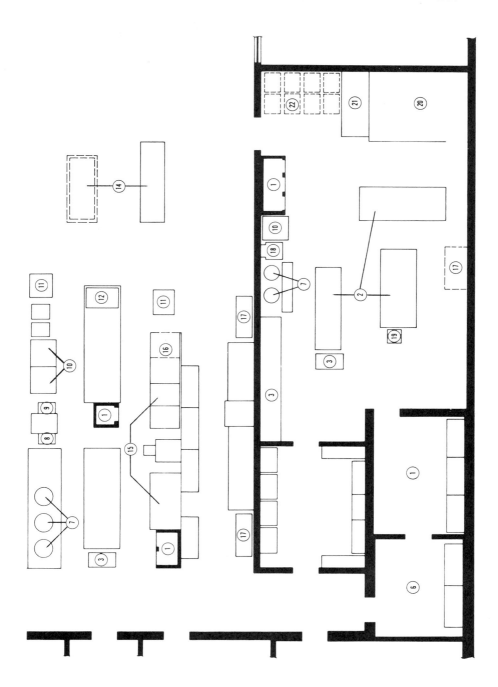

The kitchen layout for preparing the meals is basically straight-line configurations of equipment. One configuration is used for the preparation, cooking and packing of hot foods and another for the preparation and production of cold foods. This type of configuration enables the commissary to utilize assembly-line concepts for the fast production of the meals.

Typical Portion Sizes for Menu Items

Beverages
  Coffee — 4 oz
  Tea — 4 oz
  Milk — ½ pint
  Soft drinks — 4 to 6 oz
Breads, Rolls, Cereals
  Bread — 2 oz
  Cream of wheat — 4 oz
  Hot rolls — 2 oz
  Muffins — 2 cakes
  Cereals, flaked — 4 oz
  Cereals, puffed — 2 oz
  Toast — 4 oz
Casseroles, Stews, Etc.
  Baked beans — 6 oz
  Chili con carne — 6 oz
  Corned beef — 6 oz
  Corned beef hash — 6 oz
  Goulash — 6 oz
  Ham a la king — 4 oz
  Macaroni and
    cheese — 5 oz
  Meat loaf — 5 oz
  Short ribs — 12 oz
  Spaghetti — 5 oz
  Spanish rice — 5 oz
  Stews — 7 oz
  Stuffed cabbage — 4 oz
Fruits
  Canned — 4 oz
  Fresh — 4 to 6 oz
Meats
  Bacon — 5 oz
  Beef
    Roasts — 6 oz
    Steaks
      Chateaubriand — 16 oz

Filet mignon — 6 oz
Minute — 6 oz
Porterhouse — 16 oz
Salisbury — 8 oz
Sirloin — 8 oz
T-bone — 12 oz
Ham — 6 oz
Lamb chops — 10 oz
Liver — 4 oz
Pork chops — 7 oz
Sausage — 6 oz
Veal chops — 8 oz
Veal cutlets — 5 oz
Pastries, desserts, etc.
  Cakes — 2 oz
  Ice cream — 4 oz
  Pies, fruit — 8 oz
  Puddings — 5 oz
Poultry
  Chicken, fried — 8 oz
  Chicken, broiled — 8 oz
  Duck — 10 oz
  Turkey — 7 oz
Salads
  Cole slaw — 3 oz
  Chicken salad — 4 oz
  Mixed vegetable — 4 oz
  Potato — 4 oz
  Waldorf — 4 oz
Sandwiches (excluding bread)
  Beef — 4 oz
  Cheese — 2 oz
  Chicken — 2 oz
  Ham — 2 oz
  Hamburgers — 2 to 4 oz
  Turkey — 2 oz

Seafood

  Clams — 12 Little Neck

  Crabs, soft-shell — 2 crabs

  Fish — 6 to 7 oz

  Frogs' legs — 8 oz

  Lobster, half — 12 oz

  Oysters — 6 oysters

  Shrimp — 6 oz

Soups

  Cup — 6 oz

  Bowl — 8 oz

Vegetables

  Asparagus, fresh — 7 pieces

  Asparagus, tips — 5 oz

  Beans, green — 4 oz

  Beans, lima — 4 oz

  Beets — 5 oz

  Cauliflower — 5 oz

  Carrots — 5 oz

  Corn, cob — 2 ears

  Corn, kernel — 5 oz

  Potatoes — 6 oz

  Peas — 4 oz

  Spinach — 6 oz

  Squash — 4 oz

  Tomatoes — 5 oz

Information for Developing a Food Service Prospectus

A. Customer or user characteristics
1. Identification by Occupation—indicate numbers or percentage in each category.

Business people —————— Professionals ——————
Clerical workers —————— Retirees ——————
Craftsmen —————— Sales Personnel ——————
Homemakers —————— Service workers ——————
Laborers —————— Students ——————
Office workers —————— Others ——————

2. Income level—numbers or percentage of persons in each category.

Under $4000 —————— 12,000–13,999 ——————
4000–5999 —————— 14,000–15,999 ——————
5000–7999 —————— 16,000–19,999 ——————
8000–9999 —————— Over 20,000 ——————
10,000–11,999 ——————

3. Age and Sex—numbers or percentage in each age bracket and breakdown by sex.

	Male	Female
Under 5 years ——————	——————	——————
6–11 ——————	——————	——————
12–17 ——————	——————	——————
18–24 ——————	——————	——————
25–34 ——————	——————	——————
35–49 ——————	——————	——————
50–64 ——————	——————	——————
Over 65 ——————	——————	——————

4. Educational level—numbers or percentage who have completed each level.

Elementary ————————————————————
Secondary ————————————————————
College (Junior or Community) ——————————
University ——————————————————

5. Motivation for eating out—indicate or estimate percentage in each category.

Change in routine —————— Special occasions ——————
Necessity —————— Adventure ——————

Convenience _____   Entertainment _____

Business reasons _____   To get special kinds of meals _____

Social _____   Other _____

6. Spending habits—estimate average amount to be spent for each meal; may be identified by sex, age or income if desirable.

Breakfast _____   Afternoon snack _____

Mid-morning snack _____   Dinner _____

Lunch _____   After-dinner snack _____

7. Activities related to dining out—identify or estimate percentages.

Shopping _____   Entertainment events _____

Traveling or touring _____   Organized group meetings _____

Attending conventions _____   Social group meetings _____

Visiting _____   Other _____

Business _____

8. Arrival patterns—estimate percentage for each group.

Singles, male _____

Singles, female _____

Couples _____

Families _____   Average size _____

Men groups _____   Average size _____

Women groups _____   Average size _____

Mixed groups _____   Average size _____

9. Miscellaneous factors—identify and describe if related to a particular type of facility.

Ethnic backgrounds _____

_____

Food preferences _____

_____

Eating habits _____

_____

Service preferences _____

_____

Marital status _____

_____

Means of transportation _____

_____

Preferred meal periods of dining out _____

_____

Preferred days for dining out _____

_____

B. Menu characteristics
   1. Frequency of change—indicate type for each meal period.

	Breakfast	Lunch	Dinner
Completely fixed menu	_____	_____	_____
Fixed with seasonal changes	_____	_____	_____
Fixed with changing specials	_____	_____	_____
Complete daily changes	_____	_____	_____
Cyclical daily changes	_____	_____	_____
(Indicate length of cycle)			
Daily changes with standard items	_____	_____	_____

   2. Type of items—indicate for each meal.

	Breakfast	Lunch	Dinner
A la Carte	_____	_____	_____
Club or complete meal	_____	_____	_____
Combination	_____	_____	_____

   3. Extent of offerings—indicate number of items in each category for each meal.

	Breakfast	Lunch	Dinner
Appetizers	_____	_____	_____
Soups	_____	_____	_____
Salads	_____	_____	_____
Main entrees	_____	_____	_____
Sandwiches	_____	_____	_____

	Breakfast	Lunch	Dinner
Potatoes	_____	_____	_____
Vegetables	_____	_____	_____
Bread and rolls	_____	_____	_____
Desserts	_____	_____	_____
Beverages	_____	_____	_____
Other	_____	_____	_____

   4. Typical menu for each meal—include portions size for each item.

C. Service
   1. Type—indicate appropriate category.
     Service units
       Table service   _____
       Counter service   _____

Booth service _____
Combination table and counter _____
Combination table and booth _____
Combination counter and booth _____
Tray service _____
Car service _____
Room service _____
Self-service units
    Cafeteria units _____
    Buffet service _____
    Take-out service _____
    Vending units _____
  2. Standards—indicate type of material and quality.

	Material	Quality
Tablecloths	_____	_____
Napkins	_____	_____
Place mats	_____	_____
Dishware	_____	_____
Hollowware	_____	_____
Glassware	_____	_____
Flatware	_____	_____
Other _____	_____	_____

  3. Beverage service—indicate type and method.
    Non-alcoholic _____
    Alcoholic _____

D. Atmosphere
  1. Type—indicate.
    Formal _____   Cheerful _____
    Informal _____   Relaxed _____
    Intimate _____   Appealing _____
                    Other _____
  2. Special emphasis
    Exterior _____   View _____
    Interior _____   Theme _____
    Location _____   Costuming _____

E. Operational characteristics
  1. Type of ownership and organization.
    Independent owner _____   Proprietorship _____
    Chain _____   Partnership _____
    Franchise _____   Corporation _____
    Lease _____   Other _____

2. Meal periods; days and hours of operation, expected number of customers.

	Days	Hours	No. of customers
Breakfast	_____	_____	_____
Mid-morning snack	_____	_____	_____
Lunch	_____	_____	_____
Afternoon snack	_____	_____	_____
Dinner	_____	_____	_____
After-dinner snack	_____	_____	_____

3. Procedures

Purchasing _____   Waste disposal _____
Production _____   Cash _____
Service _____   Communications _____
Warewashing _____   Others _____

4. Regulatory considerations—check proposed project for compliance with:

Zoning laws _____   Liquor laws _____
Building code _____   Labor laws _____
Sanitary code _____   Other _____

Listing of Tasks Commonly Performed in Food Service Facilities

I. ACCOUNTING
  A. ANALYSIS
    1. Analyzing operating data
    2. Analyzing financial data
    3. Auditing all bills
    4. Auditing all cash in the cash system
    5. Compiling financial reports
    6. Compiling financial collection reports
    7. Compiling disbursement reports
    8. Compiling reconciliation reports
    9. Compiling statistical reports
    10. Consolidating cost data
    11. Determining costs of operation
    12. Examining accounting and control procedures to determine compliance with regulations
    13. Analyzing accounting records for useful information
    14. Studying problems and recommending action
  B. BOOKEEPING
    1. Adjusting control totals
    2. Adjusting ledger totals
    3. Approving bills and invoices
    4. Ascertaining accounts affected by transaction
    5. Assessing banquet charges
    6. Balancing control accounts
    7. Balancing disbursements
    8. Balancing ledger accounts
    9. Balancing receipts
    10. Comparing forms
    11. Correcting errors in accounts
    12. Correcting customer errors
    13. Correcting vendor errors
    14. Crediting accounts
    15. Debiting accounts
    16. Keeping records
    17. Listing charges
    18. Making journal entries
    19. Posting bills due

20. Posting bills paid
21. Posting changes to records
22. Posting data to accounts
23. Posting supply data
24. Posting details of financial transactions
25. Posting expense vouchers
26. Posting expenses
27. Posting payroll deductions
28. Posting payroll to pay records
29. Posting revenues
30. Processing bills
31. Record financial transactions
32. Recording monetary transactions
33. Recording reservations
34. Verifying daily balances against predetermined figures
35. Verifying journal entries

C. COMPUTATION
1. Aging accounts receivable
2. Computing bills
3. Computing figures for financial reports
4. Computing financial ratios
5. Computing losses
6. Computing payroll deductions
7. Computing profits
8. Computing total costs
9. Computing total percentages
10. Computing sales
11. Computing unit costs
12. Computing unit percentages
13. Counting bills
14. Determining food costs
15. Determining maintenance costs
16. Determining labor costs
17. Determining overhead costs
18. Making out payroll
19. Preparing charts and graphs (financial)
20. Preparing daily meal abstracts
21. Preparing meal recap reports
22. Proofing computations
23. Reconciling bank account
24. Totaling accounts
25. Totaling checks

D. CREDIT
    1. Accepting payments on customer accounts
    2. Analyzing delinquent accounts and recommending action
    3. Authorizing limits and charges
    4. Authorizing issuance of credit cards
    5. Collecting funds due from employees
    6. Composing collection notes to customers
    7. Determining credit ratings
    8. Determining payment methods for accounts receivable
    9. Evaluating financial standing of credit applicants
    10. Interviewing customers to determine credit problems
    11. Issuing credit cards
    12. Issuing replacement credit cards
    13. Issuing list of lost or stolen credit cards
    14. Liaison with collection agency
    15. Maintaining credit cards records
    16. Maintaining list of lost or stolen credit cards
    17. Notifying customers of credit limits
    18. Preparing delinquency notice
    19. Presenting the bill
    20. Processing accounts due
    21. Processing credit card applications
    22. Ringing-up charges on the cash register
    23. Submitting delinquent accounts to a collection agency or attorney for collection
    24. Tracing delinquents
    25. Typing receipts
    26. Verifying accounts receivable
    27. Verifying references and information on credit applications
E. DATA COLLECTION
    1. Arranging data
    2. Comparing data
    3. Collecting specific cost-distribution data
    4. Keeping employee time records
    5. Preparing financial statement
    6. Preparing balance sheet
    7. Preparing income statement
    8. Recording data
    9. Researching outstanding accounts
    10. Compiling requested accounting information

11. Tabulating food and beverage checks
12. Tabulating the number of units sold of each product

F. DISBURSING
    1. Allocating funds
    2. Cashing checks
    3. Collecting parking fees
    4. Counting money
    5. Verifying accounts
    6. Disbursing funds
    7. Drawing up budgets
    8. Issuing refunds
    9. Keeping custody of house fund
    10. Maintaining bank account
    11. Maintaining petty cash fund
    12. Making change
    13. Mailing checks
    14. Mailing cash
    15. Paying company expenditures
    16. Paying employees
    17. Preparing bank deposit
    18. Preparing cash and checks for deposit
    19. Preparing checks
    20. Preparing payroll
    21. Processing checks
    22. Processing claims
    23. Receiving incoming checks and currency
    24. Sorting coins
    25. Wrapping coins

II. CLERICAL

A. SECRETARIAL
    1. Answering letters
    2. Assembling reports
    3. Binding reports
    4. Correcting accounts
    5. Filing correspondence
    6. Filing forms
    7. Setting files
    8. Labeling files
    9. Mailing correspondence
    10. Moving files
    11. Proofreading
    12. Scheduling appointments

          13. Sorting forms
          14. Stapling reports
          15. Taking dictation
   B. FILING
           1. Filing
           2. Keeping record of calls
           3. Keeping records of correspondence
           4. Keeping records of long-distance calls placed
           5. Maintaining files
           6. Maintaining information file
           7. Maintaining output records
           8. Maintaining record of food items ordered
           9. Maintaining record of mixed drinks ordered
          10. Maintaining record of packages received
          11. Maintaining record of tardiness
          12. Maintaining record of uneaten food
          13. Maintaining record of wines ordered
          14. Maintaining capital records
          15. Maintaining indebtedness records
          16. Making indexes
          17. Recording data on unusual occurrences
          18. Retrieving requested information from files
          19. Searching files for requested information
   C. TYPING
           1. Cutting ditto master sheets
           2. Cutting stencils
           3. Drafting correspondence
           4. Drafting requisitions
           5. Duplicating documents
           6. Preparing requisitions
           7. Typing correspondence
           8. Typing memos
           9. Typing reports
          10. Typing requisitions
          11. Typing schedules
          12. Typing work-service requests
          13. Writing accident reports
          14. Writing damage reports
III. COMMUNICATION
   A. GENERAL
           1. Addressing envelopes, forms, and letters
           2. Answering phone
           3. Composing correspondence

4. Composing routine memos
5. Delivering mail to post office
6. Distributing mail
7. Drafting reports
8. Handling incoming messages
9. Handling unusual requests and inquiries
10. Issuing periodic reports of operating status
11. Issuing reports concerning financial status
12. Issuing reports of operating procedures
13. Maintaining internal communication system
14. Making daily management report
15. Making-up food and beverage report
16. Notifying employees when they must work other than scheduled periods
17. Notifying management of need for repairs
18. Opening mail
19. Picking up incoming mail
20. Preparing routine reports
21. Reporting equipment breakdown
22. Reporting maintenance needs of equipment
23. Reporting needed repairs to superior
24. Reporting unusual happenings to management
25. Reporting all accidents
26. Reporting damage
27. Sorting mail
28. Taking telephone messages
29. Transcribing from shorthand

IV. MAINTENANCE
   A. BUILDING
1. Buffing floors
2. Burning refuse
3. Changing filters
4. Checking for burnt-out lights
5. Cleaning air ducts
6. Cleaning awnings
7. Cleaning cabinets
8. Cleaning ceilings
9. Cleaning counters
10. Cleaning door glass
11. Cleaning door ventilators
12. Cleaning drawers
13. Cleaning fans
14. Cleaning marble

15. Cleaning pipes and fixtures
16. Cleaning storage bins
17. Cleaning walls
18. Cleaning windows
19. Cleaning work areas
20. Collecting trash
21. Disposing of non-combustible trash
22. Doing routine painting
23. Doing routine plumbing
24. Dusting
25. Emptying garbage
26. Emptying trash
27. Inspecting and evaluating physical condition of building
28. Inspecting to determine painting needs
29. Keeping assigned area free of spilled food
30. Maintaining hydraulic door checks
31. Mopping floors
32. Mopping stairs
33. Opening clogged drains
34. Picking up waste paper
35. Polishing floors
36. Removing stains from carpet
37. Scrubbing floor
38. Scrubbing stairs
39. Shampooing carpet
40. Sorting bottles
41. Sorting trash
42. Spraying kitchen area
43. Sweeping floor
44. Sweeping stairs
45. Vacuuming floor
46. Vacuuming stairs
47. Washing the exterior
48. Washing doors
49. Washing windows
50. Washing interior walls
51. Washing the table tops
52. Washing counter-tops
53. Washing woodwork
54. Washing shelves
55. Waxing floors
56. Waxing counters

B. EQUIPMENT
1. Adjusting sound equipment
2. Adjusting thermostatic controls
3. Assuring compliance of electrical equipment with local regulations
4. Brushing drapes, furniture, upholstery, etc.
5. Burnishing silverware
6. Calibrating equipment
7. Changing grease (fryer)
8. Checking thermostat and temperature controls
9. Cleaning artificial flowers
10. Cleaning ash urns
11. Cleaning bain marie
12. Cleaning boiler
13. Cleaning bread baskets
14. Cleaning buffet tables
15. Cleaning burnishing machine
16. Cleaning butter bowls
17. Cleaning can opener
18. Cleaning carts
19. Cleaning china
20. Cleaning chopper
21. Cleaning chopping blocks
22. Cleaning coffee urns
23. Cleaning creamer
24. Cleaning cutter boards
25. Cleaning dipper well
26. Cleaning dish-washing machine
27. Cleaning egg slicers
28. Cleaning fans
29. Cleaning filters
30. Cleaning flaming equipment
31. Cleaning food carts
32. Cleaning freezers and refrigerators
33. Cleaning fryers
34. Cleaning furnaces
35. Cleaning griddles
36. Cleaning garbage cans and trash receptacles
37. Cleaning garbage disposal
38. Cleaning grease traps
39. Cleaning grills
40. Cleaning hood
41. Cleaning ice bins

42. Cleaning ice-cream cabinet
43. Cleaning incinerator
44. Cleaning kettles
45. Cleaning light fixtures
46. Cleaning mats
47. Cleaning meat slicer
48. Cleaning milk dispenser
49. Cleaning mixers
50. Cleaning ovens
51. Cleaning pastry carts
52. Cleaning peeling machine
53. Cleaning proof boxes
54. Cleaning ranges
55. Cleaning refrigerators
56. Cleaning scales
57. Cleaning serving stations
58. Cleaning sinks
59. Cleaning steam cooker
60. Cleaning steam table
61. Cleaning stools
62. Cleaning stoves
63. Cleaning tables
64. Cleaning thermotainer
65. Cleaning toaster
66. Cleaning toilet bowls
67. Cleaning tools
68. Cleaning urinals
69. Cleaning upholstered furniture
70. Cleaning ventilator grills
71. Cleaning waffle irons
72. Cleaning wash bowls
73. Cleaning work table
74. Dusting furniture
75. Emptying ash trays
76. Filling fruit-juice dispensers
77. Filling vending machines
78. Filtering grease
79. Greasing machinery
80. Inspecting equipment
81. Maintaining refrigerating and air-conditioning equipment
82. Maintaining sound equipment
83. Making inspections of dining-room premises

84. Making inspections of kitchen equipment
85. Making inspections of store rooms
86. Moving and arranging furniture
87. Oiling machinery
88. Polishing metals
89. Removing wax
90. Scraping bakery bench
91. Scraping dishes
92. Scraping pots and pans
93. Sharpening cutting knives
94. Sorting pots and pans
95. Stocking service bar
96. Stocking vending machines
97. Vacuuming furniture
98. Vacuuming mats
99. Washing pans
100. Washing pots
101. Washing service trays

C. GROUNDS
1. Cleaning entranceways
2. Cleaning sidewalks
3. Cleaning litter outside the building
4. Picking up papers
5. Pruning shrubs and trees
6. Removing snow
7. Sweeping parking lot
8. Weeding flower beds

V. MANAGEMENT
A. CONTROLLING
1. Adjusting work loads
2. Approving service contracts
3. Approving work orders
4. Auditing beverage checks
5. Auditing food checks
6. Auditing payroll
7. Authorizing expenditures
8. Authorizing information for publication
9. Authorizing overtime
10. Authorizing payment on C.O.D. deliveries
11. Authorizing sick leave
12. Checking beverage orders
13. Checking food orders
14. Checking for adherence to control systems

15. Clearing cash registers
16. Comparing actual and budgeted figures
17. Comparing specifications
18. Comparing work performed with standards
19. Controlling costs
20. Controlling use of forms
21. Detecting employee thievery
22. Determining degree of compliance with directives
23. Determining purchasing specifications
24. Determining standards
25. Developing regulations
26. Enforcing standards
27. Establishing policy
28. Establishing standards and procedures
29. Establishing theft controls
30. Establishing wastage controls
31. Evaluating systems of internal control
32. Examining accounting records for accuracy
33. Inspecting dishes for cleanliness
34. Inspecting finished work
35. Inspecting silverware for cleanliness
36. Inspecting work
37. Installing financial controls system
38. Instituting damage controls
39. Instituting theft controls
40. Instituting waste controls
41. Making a daily report of all cash received, disbursed, and on hand
42. Preparing budgets
43. Preparing and disseminating copies of regulatory procedures
44. Proofing computations
45. Reviewing financial records
46. Reviewing operating records
47. Reviewing order to ensure accuracy
48. Reviewing proposed expenditures against budgeted amounts and report averages
49. Setting standards
50. Spot-checking entire operation
51. Standardizing recipes
52. Tasting food for palatability
53. Verifying data accuracy
54. Verifying register totals with cash turned in

55. Weighing fish
56. Weighing ingredients
57. Weighing meat
58. Weighing poultry

B. DIRECTING
   1. Assigning work
   2. Authorizing deviation from policy and standards
   3. Coordinating work
   4. Delegating work
   5. Determining work needs
   6. Developing methods and procedures
   7. Directing activities of subordinates
   8. Directing advertising campaigns
   9. Directing maintenance of building
   10. Interpreting policy to department heads
   11. Interpreting company policy to workers
   12. Planning work schedules
   13. Preparing cleaning schedules
   14. Scheduling periodic inspections and overhauls
   15. Scheduling relief periods
   16. Supervising activities of department heads

C. ORGANIZING
   1. Advising employees
   2. Assigning duties to employees
   3. Assigning responsibilities
   4. Conferring with other department heads to coordinate activities
   5. Coordinating activities of department
   6. Coordinating activities of workers
   7. Delegating authority
   8. Determining work procedures
   9. Establishing operating procedures
   10. Evaluating adequacy of managerial procedures
   11. Evaluating adequacy of financial procedures
   12. Making recommendations to management concerning accounting procedures
   13. Organizing the entire operation
   14. Planning administrative procedures
   15. Planning production
   16. Planning for surplus food utilization
   17. Preparing cleaning schedules
   18. Promoting unity among departments

D. PLANNING
1. Adjusting work schedules
2. Advising on methods and procedures for distributing operating costs
3. Altering policies as necessary
4. Altering goals as necessary
5. Altering objectives as necessary
6. Altering standards as necessary
7. Determining goals
8. Determining methods of collection of cost data
9. Determining methods of consolidation of cost data
10. Determining methods of correlation of cost data
11. Determining methods of data correlation
12. Determining methods of data collection
13. Determining personnel needs
14. Determining policy
15. Developing menus
16. Developing promotional plans
17. Developing security procedures
18. Developing theft controls
19. Developing waste controls
20. Establishing the arrangement for storage areas
21. Estimating costs
22. Forecasting company's needs
23. Planning advertising materials
24. Planning banquets
25. Planning personnel policies
26. Planning preventive maintenance programs
27. Planning promotional materials
28. Planning public relations program
29. Planning for expansion
30. Planning for financial needs
31. Planning operations
32. Recommending changes considered necessary to aid in more effective management
33. Reviewing menu
34. Seeking advice from vendors about new products
35. Selecting recipes

VI. MARKETING
A. PROMOTION
1. Acting as liaison with advertising agency
2. Approving advertising contracts
3. Approving advertising before release

4. Approving art work
5. Arranging for printing of menu
6. Arranging for publicity
7. Arranging food for attractiveness
8. Arranging merchandise display at counter
9. Checking advertisements when they appear in the media
10. Designing layout
11. Designing menu
12. Determining advertising needs
13. Dispersing advertising and promotional literature
14. Negotiating advertising contract
15. Preparing advertising materials
16. Preparing promotional materials
17. Preparing publicity releases
18. Procuring mailing lists
19. Promoting good will between the groups and the establishment
20. Purchasing advertising time and space as needed
21. Setting up sales displays
22. Stocking shelves at merchandise counter
23. Writing sales outlines for use by staff

B. PUBLIC RELATIONS
1. Conducting public relations programs
2. Directing public-opinion poll
3. Greeting important guests
4. Greeting visitors
5. Participating in community and civic affairs
6. Preparing company publication
7. Taking public-opinion polls
8. Writing news releases

C. SALES
1. Adjusting complaints
2. Arranging banquets
3. Arranging parties
4. Cleaning menus
5. Confirming reservations
6. Consulting with members of an organization to plan their function
7. Contacting organization heads to explain the available services and facilities
8. Determining guest satisfaction
9. Drawing-up contract for groups

10. Forecasting beverage demand
11. Forecasting food demand
12. Forecasting sales
13. Handling guest complaints
14. Organizing prospect files
15. Planning banquets
16. Planning parties
17. Planning details of group functions
18. Preparing menu boards
19. Presenting menu to patron
20. Pricing items
21. Relaying food order to kitchen
22. Relaying mixed-drink order to bar
23. Selecting markets
24. Selecting prospects
25. Setting prices for beverages
26. Setting prices for food items
27. Soliciting business
28. Suggesting desserts
29. Suggesting food courses
30. Suggesting mixed drinks
31. Suggesting wines
32. Taking patrons' orders
33. Welcoming guests
34. Writing contracts

VII. OPERATIONS
1. Assisting employees
2. Attaching bills
3. Attaching forms
4. Attaching labels
5. Checking bin cards
6. Checking breakage
7. Checking daily reports
8. Checking dining rooms for table set-ups
9. Checking doors
10. Checking drawers
11. Checking employees' work
12. Checking equipment operation
13. Checking food orders
14. Checking food quality
15. Checking inventories
16. Checking invoices
17. Checking orders
18. Checking par stocks

19. Checking refrigerators
20. Checking requisitions
21. Checking reservations
22. Checking sales
23. Checking side stands
24. Checking supplies of food
25. Checking supplies of china, glasses, silverware
26. Checking weights
27. Erecting displays
28. Getting materials
29. Getting tools
30. Listing needed supplies
31. Loading carts
32. Maintaining spare parts
33. Moving chairs
34. Moving tables
35. Operating accounting machines
36. Operating adding machines
37. Operating cash registers
38. Operating computing machines
39. Operating compactors
40. Operating copying machines
41. Operating dishwashers
42. Operating dumb waiter
43. Operating glasswasher
44. Operating mixers
45. Operating scrubbers
46. Operating slicers
47. Preparing menus
48. Preparing reports
49. Removing carts
50. Removing trays
51. Removing tables
52. Setting up menu boards
53. Setting up partitions
54. Taking reservations

VIII. PERSONNEL MANAGEMENT
  A. EVALUATING
    1. Checking appearance of employees
    2. Comparing work methods
    3. Counseling employees
    4. Determining personnel suitable for promotion and transfer
    5. Evaluating employee performance

    6. Evaluating supervisory and executive personnel
    7. Evaluating workers
    8. Examining work
    9. Inspecting employees for neatness
   10. Keeping personnel records
   11. Maintaining personnel records
   12. Making recommendations regarding promotions, etc.
   13. Observing employee performance
   14. Testing employees eligible for promotion
   15. Writing job descriptions
   16. Writing job specifications

B. MOTIVATING
    1. Authorizing pay raises
    2. Conducting time and motion studies
    3. Developing incentive programs
    4. Granting pay raises
    5. Maintaining harmony among workers
    6. Making salary adjustments
    7. Motivating workers
    8. Promoting and transferring personnel

C. NEGOTIATING
    1. Acting as liaison between labor and management
    2. Bargaining with unions
    3. Determining pay scale
    4. Developing salary and wage scales
    5. Establishing and maintaining grievance procedures
    6. Establishing pay rates
    7. Establishing pension and insurance plans
    8. Establishing workmen's compensation policies
    9. Interpreting union contracts
   10. Negotiating contracts
   11. Representing company in negotiating labor agreements
   12. Resolving complaints
   13. Resolving personnel problems at supervisory and executive level
   14. Settling arguments
   15. Settling grievances

D. STAFFING
    1. Administering aptitude tests
    2. Administering personality tests
    3. Discharging employees
    4. Determining staff requirements

     5. Establishing work schedules
     6. Hiring employees
     7. Hiring executive personnel
     8. Interpreting union policies and procedures to employees
     9. Interviewing applicants
   10. Notifying applicants of rejection
   11. Notifying applicants of selection
   12. Organizing recruiting procedures
   13. Organizing selection procedures
   14. Recording and evaluating information about job applicants
   15. Regulating workloads
   16. Selecting applicants for further consideration
   17. Testing job applicants
   18. Verifying information on job applicants
   19. Verifying references

E. TRAINING
     1. Acquiring knowledge of requirements for all jobs
     2. Developing training manuals
     3. Evaluating performance and progress of trainees
     4. Forecasting training needs
     5. Informing job applicants of company and union policies
     6. Interpreting standards to workers
     7. Organizing training procedures
     8. Orienting new employees
     9. Preparing training materials
   10. Revising job descriptions
   11. Training employees

IX. PRODUCTION
A. PHYSICAL PRODUCT
     1. Adding ingredients
     2. Applying egg wash
     3. Arranging cold-meat dishes
     4. Baking meat
     5. Baking biscuits
     6. Baking bread
     7. Baking buns
     8. Baking cakes
     9. Baking cookies
   10. Baking fish
   11. Baking fowl

12. Baking lamb
13. Baking pastries
14. Baking muffins
15. Baking pies
16. Baking rolls
17. Baking shellfish
18. Baking sweet rolls
19. Baking vegetables
20. Barbecuing meat
21. Barbecuing fowl
22. Batter-dipping meat
23. Batter-dipping fish
24. Batter-dipping fruit
25. Batter-dipping shellfish
26. Beating ingredients
27. Boiling beef
28. Boiling eggs
29. Boiling fish
30. Boiling fowl
31. Boiling lamb
32. Boiling shellfish
33. Boiling vegetables
34. Boning meat
35. Boning fowl
36. Braising meat
37. Breading meat
38. Breading fish
39. Breading shellfish
40. Brewing coffee
41. Brewing tea
42. Broiling fish
43. Broiling fowl
44. Broiling meat
45. Carving butter
46. Carving meat
47. Carving fowl
48. Chopping eggs
49. Chopping meat
50. Chopping fish
51. Chopping fowl
52. Chopping fruit
53. Chopping vegetables
54. Chopping nuts

55. Chopping shellfish
56. Cracking nuts
57. Creaming vegetables
58. Cutting meat
59. Cutting bread
60. Cutting fish
61. Cutting fowl
62. Cutting fruit
63. Cutting pastries
64. Cutting vegetables
65. Decorating pastry
66. Deep-frying meat
67. Deep-frying fish
68. Deep-frying fowl
69. Deep-frying vegetables
70. Deep-frying shellfish
71. Designing decorated foods
72. Designing artistic food arrangements
73. Developing new recipes
74. Dicing meat
75. Dicing fowl
76. Dicing fruit
77. Dicing vegetables
78. Dicing shellfish
79. Draining bottles
80. Draining cans
81. Drawing tap beer
82. Dusting foods with flour
83. Examining foods
84. Estimating ingredients
85. Fashioning pastry decorations
86. Fileting meat and fish
87. Filling coffee pots
88. Filling creamers
89. Filling ice bins
90. Filling milk dispenser
91. Filling sugar bowls
92. Filling vending machines
93. Filling water pitchers
94. Frosting cakes
95. Frying meat
96. Frying fish
97. Frying fowl

98. Frying vegetables
99. Frying shellfish
100. Garnishing cold-meat trays
101. Garnishing entrees
102. Garnishing mixed drinks
103. Garnishing salads
104. Grating cheese
105. Greasing pans
106. Grilling meat
107. Grilling fish
108. Grilling fowl
109. Grilling shellfish
110. Grinding cheese
111. Grinding coffee beans
112. Grinding fruit
113. Grinding meat
114. Grinding vegetables
115. Grinding spices
116. Making appetizers
117. Making broth
118. Making canapes
119. Making candy
120. Making casseroles
121. Making chili
122. Making chocolate
123. Making chowders
124. Making coffee
125. Making cold sauces
126. Making custards
127. Making desserts
128. Making doughnuts
129. Making fountain drinks
130. Making fritters
131. Making fruit salads
132. Making garnishes
133. Making gravies
134. Making gelatin salads
135. Making hot chocolate
136. Making ice cream
137. Making ice coffee
138. Making iced tea
139. Making icings
140. Making Jello

184. Portioning vegetables
185. Posting menus
186. Pouring batter
187. Pouring drinks
188. Preparing appetizers
189. Preparing dough
190. Preparing cake batter
191. Preparing cocktail sauces
192. Preparing cooked cereal
193. Preparing dessert fruits
194. Preparing flaming desserts
195. Preparing fountain desserts
196. Preparing fruit compotes
197. Preparing hash
198. Preparing pie fillings
199. Preparing shellfish for service
200. Preparing souffles
201. Preparing sweet roll dough
202. Preparing whipped cream
203. Removing bones
204. Removing strings
205. Roasting meat
206. Roasting fish
207. Roasting fowl
208. Seasoning food
209. Scooping ice cream
210. Scoring meats
211. Shaping fowl
212. Shaping meat
213. Shaping shellfish
214. Shelling shellfish
215. Shelling vegetables
216. Slicing bread
217. Slicing cheese
218. Slicing cold meat
219. Slicing eggs
220. Slicing pickles
221. Steaming meat
222. Steaming fowl
223. Steaming shellfish
224. Stewing fish
225. Stewing fruit
226. Stewing meat

227. Stewing poultry
228. Stewing vegetables
229. Straining vegetables
230. Stuffing celery
231. Stuffing fish
232. Stuffing vegetables
233. Tenderizing meat
234. Thawing frozen foods
235. Toasting bread
236. Traying butter
237. Trimming meat
238. Trimming fish
239. Trimming fruit
240. Trimming vegetables
241. Turning wines
242. Tying roasts
243. Washing fish
244. Washing fruit
245. Washing leafy vegetables
246. Washing shellfish
247. Whipping foods
248. Wrapping sandwiches

B. FACILITIES

1. Adjusting equipment
2. Adjusting sound equipment
3. Adjusting thermostatic controls
4. Adjusting ventilating equipment
5. Breaking-down serving station
6. Breaking-down set-ups
7. Buffing floors
8. Buffing silverware
9. Brushing furniture
10. Cleaning air ducts
11. Cleaning artificial plants
12. Cleaning ash trays
13. Cleaning ceilings
14. Cleaning condiment containers
15. Cleaning counter
16. Cleaning dining tables
17. Cleaning glass
18. Cleaning filters
19. Cleaning fixtures
20. Cleaning hollowware

21. Cleaning machinery
22. Cleaning marble
23. Cleaning out-door furniture
24. Cleaning bathroom fixtures
25. Cleaning sinks
26. Cleaning toilets
27. Cleaning upholstered furniture
28. Cleaning urinals
29. Cleaning wash basins
30. Cleaning windows
31. Clearing the table
32. Collecting trash
33. Drying glassware
34. Dusting
35. Emptying ash trays
36. Emptying garbage
37. Emptying trash
38. Fashioning table decorations
39. Filling dispensing machines
40. Folding napkins
41. Inspecting and maintaining furniture
42. Maintaining refrigerating and air-conditioning equipment
43. Maintaining sound equipment
44. Mopping floors
45. Moving tables
46. Opening clogged drains
47. Picking up and removing trays
48. Picking up waste paper
49. Polishing floors
50. Polishing glassware
51. Racking china
52. Racking glasses
53. Racking silverware
54. Removing food
55. Removing trays
56. Rinsing china
57. Rinsing glasses
58. Rinsing silverware
59. Scraping food from dirty dishes
60. Sculpturing blocks of ice
61. Setting the table
62. Setting-up decorations

63. Sorting china
64. Sorting silverware
65. Stacking dishes by catagory
66. Sterilizing silverware
67. Washing dishes
68. Washing glasses
69. Washing silverware
70. Washing table tops
71. Wiping glasses
72. Wiping silverware
73. Wrapping silverware

C. SERVICE

1. Answering questions
2. Arranging for credit for guest
3. Arranging for special services
4. Checking valuables
5. Discussing food courses
6. Discussing mixed drinks
7. Discussing wines
8. Entertaining
9. Ladling sauces
10. Ladling soups
11. Opening doors for guests
12. Seating guests
13. Serving breads
14. Serving beer
15. Serving butter
16. Serving canapes
17. Serving from chafing dish at table
18. Serving cocktails
19. Serving coffee
20. Serving dessert
21. Serving fountain drinks
22. Serving juices both fruit and vegetable
23. Serving milk
24. Serving salad
25. Serving sandwiches
26. Serving tea
27. Serving vegetables
28. Serving water
29. Serving wine
30. Tasting wine

X. PURCHASING
  A. ORDERING
    1. Authorizing purchases and expenditures
    2. Collecting orders from the various departments and delivering purchases
    3. Comparing orders
    4. Comparing specifications
    5. Compiling request for materials
    6. Consolidating request for materials
    7. Forwarding requests for materials
    8. Ordering clean linen
    9. Ordering supplies
    10. Purchasing bar equipment
    11. Purchasing bar supplies
    12. Purchasing beer
    13. Purchasing building and maintenance supplies, etc.
    14. Purchasing cleaning equipment
    15. Purchasing clerical supplies
    16. Purchasing dairy products
    17. Purchasing dining-room equipment
    18. Purchasing dining-room supplies
    19. Purchasing kitchen equipment
    20. Purchasing kitchen supplies
    21. Purchasing linens
    22. Purchasing liquor
    23. Purchasing meats
    24. Purchasing non-alcoholic beverages
    25. Purchasing produce
    26. Purchasing staples
    27. Purchasing wines
    28. Requisitioning supplies and services
  B. RECEIVING
    1. Examining incoming orders for quality
    2. Moving containers, opening containers
    3. Receiving clean linen supplies
    4. Receiving clean uniforms from laundry
    5. Unpacking items
    6. Verifying incoming orders of supplies
  C. STORING
    1. Inspecting food supplies
    2. Iventorying bar equipment
    3. Inventorying bar supplies
    4. Inventorying beer

       4. Preparing surfaces for painting
       5. Refinishing floors
       6. Removing wall paper
       7. Repairing carpets
       8. Repairing drapes
       9. Replacing broken tiles
     10. Replacing faucet washers
     11. Replacing floor tile
     12. Scraping paint
     13. Varnishing surfaces

B. EQUIPMENT
       1. Repairing electrical fixtures
       2. Repairing refrigerating and air-conditioning equipment
       3. Repairing silverware
       4. Repairing sound equipment
       5. Repairing thermostats
       6. Replacing bearings
       7. Replating silverware
       8. Reupholstering worn or damaged furniture

XII. TRANSPORTATION

A. NON-VEHICULAR
       1. Delivering messages
       2. Removing empty bottles
       3. Removing garbage
       4. Removing trash
       5. Transporting foods from storage area to production area
       6. Transporting food to serving counters
       7. Transporting supplies from storage to production area
       8. Transporting used utensils from dining room to washing area
       9. Transporting utensils to serving counter

Index

NOTES

NOTES

Date Due